January–April 20⁖

Day by Day
with
God

Rooting women's lives in the Bible

The Bible Reading Fellowship
Christina Press
Abingdon/Tunbridge Wells

The Bible Reading Fellowship
15 The Chambers, Vineyard
Abingdon OX14 3FE
brf.org.uk

The Bible Reading Fellowship (BRF) is a Registered Charity (233280)

ISBN 978 0 85746 614 3
All rights reserved

This edition © 2017 Christina Press and The Bible Reading Fellowship
Cover image © Thinkstock

Distributed in Australia by:
MediaCom Education Inc, PO Box 610, Unley, SA 5061
Tel: 1 800 811 311 | admin@mediacom.org.au

Distributed in New Zealand by:
Scripture Union Wholesale, PO Box 760, Wellington
Tel: 04 385 0421 | suwholesale@clear.net.nz

Acknowledgements
Scripture quotations taken from the Holy Bible, New Living Translation, copyright ©
1996, 2004, 2007, 2013. Used by permission of Tyndale House Publishers, Inc., Carol
Stream, Illinois 60188. All rights reserved. • Scripture quotations taken from The New
Revised Standard Version of the Bible, Anglicised Edition, copyright © 1989, 1995 by
the Division of Christian Education of the National Council of the Churches of Christ
in the USA, are used by permission. All rights reserved. • Scripture quotations from the
Good News Bible published by The Bible Societies/HarperCollins Publishers Ltd, UK
© American Bible Society 1966, 1971, 1976, 1992, used with permission. • Scripture
quotations taken from The Holy Bible, New International Version (Anglicised edition),
copyright © 1979, 1984, 2011 by Biblica. Used by permission of Hodder & Stoughton
Publishers, an Hachette UK company. All rights reserved. 'NIV' is a registered
trademark of Biblica. UK trademark number 1448790. • Scripture quotations taken
from the Holy Bible, English Standard Version, published by HarperCollins Publishers,
© 2001 Crossway Bibles, a division of Good News Publishers. Used by permission.
All rights reserved. • Scripture taken from the Holy Bible, New International Reader's
Version®. Copyright © 1996, 1998, Biblica. All rights reserved throughout the world.
Used by permission of Biblica. • Extracts from CEB copyright © 2011 by Common
English Bible. • Scripture quotations from THE MESSAGE. Copyright © by Eugene H.
Peterson 1993, 1994, 1995. Used by permission of NavPress Publishing Group. •
Scripture quotations from the Contemporary English Version. New Testament ©
American Bible Society 1991, 1992, 1995. Old Testament © American Bible Society
1995. Anglicisations © British & Foreign Bible Society 1996. Used by permission. •
Scripture quotations taken from the Amplified® Bible, Copyright © 1954, 1958, 1962,
1964, 1965, 1987 by The Lockman Foundation. Used by permission. (www.Lockman.
org). • The Living Bible copyright © 1971 by Tyndale House Foundation. Used by
permission of Tyndale House Publishers Inc., Carol Stream, Illinois 60188. All rights
reserved. • Scripture taken from the New Century Version®. Copyright © 2005 by
Thomas Nelson. Used by permission. All rights reserved.

Printed by Gutenberg Press, Tarxien, Malta

Day by Day
with
God

Edited by **Ali Herbert** and **Jill Rattle**   January–April 2018

Writers in this issue

Diana Archer works as a freelance writer, editor and trainer. She runs Tastelife (**www.tastelifeuk.org**), a charity set up to help people break free from eating disorders. Tastelife trains people to run a community course, which gives sufferers from eating disorders, and their supporters, hope and tools for recovery.

Tania Vaughan is a teacher of God's word. She is passionate about helping women go deeper with God. Tania shares her battle with depression and destructive relationships on her website, **www.taniavaughan.com**.

Rosemary Green has four adult offspring and 14 grandchildren, aged between 30 and eleven. She and her husband live in Abingdon, where she is involved in ministry among seniors in her local church.

Bex Lewis is a southerner 'up north' as Senior Lecturer in Digital Marketing at Manchester Metropolitan University. She is passionate about helping people engage with the digital age in a positive way, and is the author of *Raising Children in a Digital Age: Enjoying the best and avoiding the worst* (Lion Hudson, 2014).

Victoria Byrne serves on church healing teams and loves encouraging others. She is married and works on the pastoral staff at her Twickenham church. She writes and blogs regularly on life and faith.

Esther Kuku has a career in broadcast journalism and PR that spans 20 years. She is married with four children, including two stepchildren. On Saturday mornings, Esther presents *The Family Hour* on the radio station Premier Gospel.

Claire Musters is an author, a speaker and an editor; she is also a mum, a pastor's wife, a worship leader and a school governor. Claire's passion is to help others draw closer to God. Her latest books include *Insight into Burnout*, co-written with Chris Ledger (CWR, 2017), and *Taking off the Mask: Learning to live authentically* (Authentic Media, 2017).

Cathy Madavan is the author of *Digging for Diamonds: Finding treasure in the messiness of life* (Authentic Media, 2015). She speaks at events across the UK and is part of the Spring Harvest Planning Group. She lives on the south coast with her husband Mark (a church leader) and their two teenage girls.

Amy Boucher Pye is the author of *The Living Cross: Exploring God's gift of forgiveness and new life* (BRF, 2016) and the award-winning *Finding Myself in Britain: Our search for faith, home & true identity* (Authentic Media, 2015). She enjoys running the Woman Alive book club and speaking at churches. She blogs at **www.amyboucherpye.com**.

Ali Herbert and Jill Rattle write...

Jill: I've recently read *Eat This Book: The art of spiritual reading* (Hodder & Stoughton, 2008) by Eugene H. Peterson (author of *THE MESSAGE*). The title comes from Revelation 10:9, where the angel holds a scroll in his hand and urges John to 'take it and eat it'. In his book Peterson urges Christians to 'consume', 'chew', 'savour' and 'digest' the scriptures, allowing the glorious revelation of God to transform us more and more into the image of Jesus. And this amazing 'meal' includes the tougher bits, not just those that are easy to swallow.

So, in this issue, we've set ourselves the challenge to 'consume' a couple of the harder books of the Bible. Near the beginning and at the end, Rosemary Green opens up for us the letter to the Hebrews. This is a section of the New Testament that some of us bypass as rather too difficult. And yet, as Rosemary shows us, if we are prepared to engage with it, we will understand more of who Jesus is and increase our wonder at having a relationship with him.

In April, Amy Boucher Pye takes us through the Old Testament book of Zechariah and shows us how God redeems and restores his people – a foretaste and a foretelling of the saving work of Jesus.

There is no doubt what the outcome of us consuming, chewing, savouring and digesting the scriptures will be – we will be changed!

Ali: To help us continue the theme of pressing into the Bible and discovering what it means for our lives, we are delighted to welcome Tania Vaughan and Esther Kuku as new writers.

In January, Tania explores how we can be hungry to read the Bible – and whets our appetite for the blessings we receive as we do. A little later on, in March, Esther looks at how we might spread some of that delight, nourishment and good news to those with whom we share our lives: our families, churches and communities.

As we begin the new year and fill up with the goodness of scripture, maybe we could cultivate an 'attitude of gratitude' using the children's mealtime prayer: 'For every cup and plateful, dear Lord we're very grateful!' Enjoy!

Resolutions – the ten commandments

Diana Archer writes:

Happy New Year! It's that time again. It's almost impossible to resist making a New Year's resolution or two. A fresh year and a fresh start can feel so good. Some people do actually succeed with their resolutions – perhaps you are one of them. Of course, statistics tell us that the vast majority of us are overenthusiastic and have dropped our resolutions by nine days into January – not very encouraging.

Yet a new start is what God offers us time and time again, unlimited by the date on the calendar. His mercies 'are new every morning' (Lamentations 3:23). No matter how this new year feels for you, no matter what you are thinking, no matter what your situation, God in Jesus offers forgiveness, strength, purpose, power and his presence by his Spirit to go into the year with you. This does not depend on you winding up the willpower to change your life. It doesn't depend on a list of 'if onlys' – 'If only I had more discipline'; 'If only I had what I want'; 'If only I had another life'; 'If only I was a different me.' God's presence with you is dependent on the fact that he loves you. There is nothing you can do to change that.

So, rather than making wild resolutions that may be doomed, why not set off into the year holding Jesus' hand and depending on him? I know that sounds rather obvious, but it is extraordinary how the seduction of doing things our way can subtly distract us from utterly surrendering to Jesus' way.

This is why we are going to spend some time looking at the ten commandments – not as resolutions but as God's way of doing things. It could actually be that he knows best how to make life work. Will we dare to trust him?

If I only had a heart

'I will give you a new heart, and I will put a new spirit in you. I will take out your stony, stubborn heart and give you a tender, responsive heart.' (NLT)

When the Israelites first heard the ten commandments, they had been wandering in the desert for a while, having escaped, as a nation, from slavery in Egypt. They were on their way to freedom, but God had some work to do in them before they were ready to take on life in the promised land. Those 40 years in the wilderness were to prove vital in the nation's learning about God, about themselves and about how to live as a nation who belonged to Yahweh, the God of Israel.

Most of us are very familiar with the ten commandments – or at least know some of them – and they are the bedrock upon which the laws of Western society are built. But when Moses first came out of the mist on Mount Sinai carrying commandments to live by, they were revolutionary. They gave the fledgling nation a framework for formation that was in deep contrast to the established nations around them. The most revolutionary concept was that the God who gave the commandments, above all else, wanted a loving relationship with his people.

The words from Ezekiel draw this out. Yes, God is concerned that his name has been maligned. Yes, he is distraught about Israel's behaviour. But this is only because he cares utterly for his people and wants to be in relationship with them. He longs to bless them and their land, but he can't while they are turned away from him. So he offers to remake them, and bring them to life from the inside out.

It is so easy to think that we can do it all ourselves. I fall into that trap a dozen times a day. But the commandments are about relationships, not about ticking off a list. And for this, I definitely need some help.

If you described the state of your heart today, how much would be stony, and how much would be responsive?

DIANA ARCHER

Mission: Impossible

'I am the Lord your God, who rescued you from the land of Egypt, the place of your slavery. You must not have any other god but me.' (NLT)

Here we go with the first commandment. If I were God, I would probably make it number one like he has. I would know that I was the only God, because I was God. So my dearly beloved people would need to know that first of all.

But wait. This isn't just about facts. It isn't just that the God of Israel was reminding the Israelites that they were to choose him and not any of the gods in the surrounding cultures. It isn't even just about the tendency we have as human beings to find other things to put in the place of God – other things to believe in, put our trust in, assign greatness to and allow to dominate our lives; other things to worship; other things to focus on.

It's also about what God says before he introduces commandment number one. This commandment is based on that relationship principle we thought about yesterday. The God who asks that we put him first has already put us first. He has rescued us from the place of our slavery.

For the Israelites, this meant Egypt, where they were the subject nation, without freedom. For us, this means the days before we knew Jesus as Saviour, without freedom. We have experienced the ultimate rescue – from sin, death and a life without God. So when God asks us to have no other gods than him, he is asking for a response to the love he has already shown us. God is not a despot or stern headmaster, demanding an unreasonable allegiance. He is the God who loves and has saved us, before we even knew we needed rescuing.

So don't beat yourself up for the times you have indeed put other things in place of God. Say sorry, of course. But then focus on discovering how much you are loved. Your response to that is what God is looking for.

DIANA ARCHER

What has your heart?

'You must not make for yourself an idol of any kind or an image of anything in the heavens or on the earth or in the sea. You must not bow down to them or worship them, for I, the Lord your God, am a jealous God.' (NLT)

Over the centuries, Christians have interpreted this second commandment in a variety of ways, from stripping churches of any semblance of an image to banning all and any art forms. The nations around Israel at the time the commandments were given had many images of their gods, big and small. The same is still true of many non-Christian religions today. But again, this isn't God being a bit petty and not wanting any competition.

This second commandment, just like all the others, is because God loves us. He made us with the ability to worship; it comes naturally to us – we simply do. What we worship, however, is a different matter entirely. It may be the statue of another godlike figure. But it may be our careers, our family, our happiness, our children or our status. It may be how we look. It may be the approval of others. Many of these are very physical, tangible things, which we can make ourselves, just like a statue. They can be very seductive, therefore, and look like they are worth our worship.

But these things are not God. They are definitely not worth our elevating them to something we live for. These temporal things do not love us completely; they are limited; they cannot represent God. Only God is God, and it is extraordinary that we choose to cause him the pain of jealousy by running after idols.

These idols are not good for us or our families either, setting up consequences that rebound down generations. But when we realise they are there, and tear them down, and return to the God who made us and loves us – then he blesses us for years and years and years.

Often we don't see that we are worshipping idols in some area of our lives. Can you ask God to show you them?

DIANA ARCHER

Swearing honestly

'You must not misuse the name of the Lord your God. The Lord will not let you go unpunished if you misuse his name.' (NLT)

Frankly, in our Western culture, this is a tough one. We seem to be surrounded by people who constantly use the name of the Lord our God as a swear word, a fill-in word, a word to say when things go wrong, or things go right, or for any reason at all – any reason except to honour God. For those of us who spend our time mainly within a Christian context, it is not so prevalent. But those who are in the mainstream of society find that few hold back from using the word 'God' in all sorts of ways.

However, this commandment is not only about swearing; it is also about using the name of God to back up things you don't mean, or promises you can't keep. But it is generally swearing that pops into people's minds first of all. Contrast the way the Jews will not even speak the name of God, because they have such enormous reverence for it. God is precious to them, and so holy that they would not dream of uttering his name aloud.

Where does that leave us? Do we have some repenting to do for using the name of God carelessly? How can we use the name of God in positive ways, so that those around us are attracted to him? Rather than having a don't-say-it mentality, how can we speak the name of God in ways that bring him honour, or hint of our love for him? How can we stir curiosity about God just by the way we say his name?

How do you best talk about Jesus?

DIANA ARCHER

Do you dare to rest?

'Remember to observe the Sabbath day by keeping it holy. You have six days each week for your ordinary work, but the seventh day is a Sabbath day of rest dedicated to the Lord your God.' (NLT)

Here is another commandment that has had a vast range of interpretations over the years. Some of our great-grandmothers sat in the front room and forbade all games and frivolity on Sundays; the Keep Sunday Special campaign still tries to limit Sunday trading in the UK; in 1924 Eric Liddell refused to run in the heats for his favoured 100 metres at the Olympics on a Sunday. Yet now on Sundays many of us happily shop, go out for meals and participate in sport – as well as going to church services.

I have no intention of delving into the debate here. It seems to me that the important thing is not what you do, but why you do it. If we are working on the glorious assumption that the commandments are based on a relationship of love with a good Creator, then a Sabbath day of rest must begin there. It was, after all, Jesus who said the Sabbath was made for our benefit, rather than us for the benefit of it (Mark 2:27). This is not about keeping a rule that we can argue over. It is about trusting God enough to keep a special part of the week just for relating to him. It is about trusting God enough to stop striving for ourselves and know that he will provide. It is about trusting God enough to put him first and relax in his presence. It is about stopping, giving God time to work in our lives and aligning the rest of our lives with his purposes too. It is deeply countercultural, even anarchic, as we create a different rhythm to the week. It is about reflecting whose image we are made in – and resting like he did.

When is your Sabbath rest? How do you know?

DIANA ARCHER

Respecting parents

'Honour your father and mother. Then you will live a long, full life in the land the Lord your God is giving you.' (NLT)

This fifth commandment turns our focus to the way we treat others. For here, in God's foundational guidelines for living, we learn that we cannot divide our relationship to God from our relationship to others. As Jesus summed it up, '"You must love the Lord your God with all your heart, all your soul, and all your mind." This is the first and greatest commandment. A second is equally important: "Love your neighbour as yourself"' (Matthew 22:37–39).

The overwhelming love that is to be the hallmark of our relationship with God is supposed to spill over into our relationships with others. Where is it to begin? With our parents. Some of us do this instinctively – our parents are beloved, we are grateful to them and they are undemanding. It is a delight to care for them. However, for others, honouring a father or mother is no picnic. There may be the sadness of dysfunctional relationships; or sickness, hurt and misunderstandings; or the darkness of abuse. In these cases, purposing good for the people who brought us up may be very challenging. It may be impossible. Perhaps we can still pray for them.

My mum is bravely coping with increasing dementia. Her family, myself included, are learning how to honour her in new ways, most of which she will never appreciate, notice or remember. But the commandment links honouring parents with long life – maybe because stable family relationships produce a network for a stable nation. At least we can return the favour of care to those who cared for us. The complex and sometimes negative feelings we may carry towards our parents are no reason not to do loving things for them. If that's you, now may be the time to talk about those feelings to your Father in heaven, who loves you perfectly.

Read Matthew 15:1–4. What does honouring your parents mean for you, even if they are not alive any more?

DIANA ARCHER

Killing softly

'You must not murder.' (NLT)

Well, this one seems fairly straightforward: no murdering. Most societies agree with this, and punish those who do it. Most recognise that taking life away from another is not an expression of love. However, it still needs saying today, just as it did when Israel first heard it. They were surrounded by cultures that included child sacrifice as a norm, and used violence as a legitimate way to end an argument. This was the God of Israel's new gold standard for how to treat others: do not take life away from them.

I do know this is a massive subject, including whether we can go to war, protect our families, assist suicide, act in self-defence or kill animals. This is not to mention wrestling with the theological problem of a God who tells us not to murder, but then sends his chosen people into a land they have to take by force.

I acknowledge all that, and I encourage you to engage with these issues, if you haven't before. But for most of us, most of the time, we are faced with other ways of 'taking life'.

In the Matthew 5 passage, Jesus makes it abundantly clear that the same motivation to murder is present in being angry with someone, or designating them stupid, or wishing them ill. It makes sense that these are on the same spectrum as actual murder, because they are destructive and lacking in love. Doing them does not stem from wanting the best for the other person, but rather destruction.

We have probably all been on the receiving end of this, even if it was just being spoken ill of. We know it hurts. We have probably all been on the perpetrating end as well. We know it is dangerous and unloving. So let's resist it.

Is anger ever OK? What is the difference between the sort of anger Jesus is talking about and the sort that God feels?

DIANA ARCHER

Emergency stop

'You must not commit adultery.' (NLT)

Now God applies the gold standard of loving each other to the marriage relationship. Like honouring parents, faithfulness within marriages makes for stable, constructive societies. Moreover, the committed relationship of marriage is given the highest respect by the scriptures, as it illustrates the relationship between Jesus Christ and his bride, the Church. This isn't simply a convenient way to organise society, but rather a reflection, albeit a pale one, of the relationship between the perfectly loving Bridegroom and his beloved – us. It could not be given a higher status. This comparison runs throughout the biblical story – from the covenant promises God makes to Abraham, to the mixture of joy and heartache expressed through the prophets as God longs for his people to love him as he loves them, to the tender love in Song of Songs – right through to the glorious union of Christ and bride at the end of all things.

No wonder adultery is such a bad thing. It's not just about a broken promise between two people. It's also about the damage done to marriage, the most important illustration of God's loving relationship with us.

Nonetheless, many of us experience the pain of this damage, and comparing it to crucial, and true, theological understandings is little help then, whether we are being adulterous or being wronged. If you are the former, may I respectfully suggest you slam your foot on the brake and stop. God knows why you started; now stop and trust him with your heart's desires. Stop trying to fix your life yourself. Get help. If you are the latter, you are so close to God's heart. He feels your pain. He will restore you.

Read Hosea 6:1–3 again. God is utterly faithful to you. He forgives you and can help you to forgive.

Lord, lead me forward in your good ways. Care for me and help me.

DIANA ARCHER

Taking

'You must not steal.' (NLT)

There is so much wrong with stealing. It's such a nasty thing to do – such an anti-loving thing. Again, we know it doesn't work as a way to organise society, as everyone running round taking everyone else's stuff isn't sustainable. But it's mainly love that gets left behind.

Our neighbours had a break-in recently. They lost various goods and items of sentimental value, and they had to replace shattered windows. But the worst thing was that they felt violated. We all know this feeling: 'That was mine! How could you just take it without asking? I feel trampled on, outraged and somehow lessened.' This doesn't only apply to stuff. All sorts of things can be stolen, like reputations, or honour, or ideas, or happiness, or even people and relationships. It leaves the victim feeling impotent, sad and angry; quite the opposite of loved.

These are hard things to come to terms with and forgive. We understand deeply why God asks us not to do them. It may be appropriate to take action against the perpetrators, as well as working on forgiveness. Or perhaps we have been the ones doing the stealing. If that is so, then today is the day to put it right if we can. Today is certainly the day to repent and do life differently.

There are also bigger battles to be fought which need our involvement. There is so much stealing on community, national and international levels that we need to stand up in Jesus' name and do something about it. There is human trafficking. There is poverty. There is climate change. There is the elderly lady down the road who needs protection against con artists…

Don't let anything steal away God's calling on your life.

DIANA ARCHER

Speaking truth

'You must not testify falsely against your neighbour.' (NLT)

In Micah 6:8 we read, 'He has shown you, O mortal, what is good. And what does the Lord require of you? To act justly and to love mercy and to walk humbly with your God.'

I'm told we live in a post-truth era. This refers to our tolerant, rejecting-of-absolutes, relativist society in the West, where worth is judged by feelings and personal beliefs. We are, apparently, not into truth any more. This does not bode well. You can't build well without truth. There doesn't seem to be any alternative to truth, except for lies.

Nothing works without truth, certainly not the law or justice. We depend on finding out the truth in order to run our court system with fairness. Morality can't function without truth – neither in society in general nor in our own lives. So the injunction not to 'testify falsely' is vital for community and individuals to thrive.

It is hopefully unlikely that we would lie in a court of law – we would rightly be penalised if so as it can lead to disastrous miscarriages of justice. In Jesus' case, false witnesses were instrumental in condemning him to death. Lack of truth can be that catastrophic.

It is perhaps more likely that we are tempted to bend the truth about our 'neighbours' – to put them down slightly, or subtly imply untrue things about them. Or maybe we keep quiet when we should stand up for them – in the canteen at work, in the staffroom or in the supermarket queue.

It just won't do. These little compromises with the truth stain our souls and open a door for more. They betray insecurities within us that need exposing to the God of truth. He is 'the way, the truth, and the life' (John 14:6, NLT). Walk with him.

Post-truth? No! We are people of the truth. Lord, guard our hearts and mouths from lies.

DIANA ARCHER

Wanting

'You must not covet your neighbour's house. You must not covet your neighbour's wife, male or female servant, ox or donkey, or anything else that belongs to your neighbour.' (NLT)

This tenth commandment is so good for us. It covers all the stuff others have that we might want. It covers relationships, lifestyles, possessions, livelihoods and travel – the whole lot. It tells us not to want them.

This is easier said than done. We know it makes sense, but it is horribly easy to fall into wanting. We are all flawed, and it is tricky not to want what other people have. We feel holes in our souls, and we think they will be filled by what we see. Before we know it, the 'if onlys' have crept in, and our dissatisfaction increases.

Western society feeds off wanting. Advertising is designed to convince us that we are lacking. We must buy, possess, accumulate. 'The one with the most stuff wins' is the motivating slogan. Or perhaps it is the crushing power of images on social media that feeds this wanting.

I work with people drowning under pressure to be and look a certain way, and it messes with their heads to a frightening degree. Eating disorders are on the rise as the 'thin is beautiful/happy' message still holds sway.

It is time to find a better way, not just for us but for our communities. Comparisons with others are deadly and lead nowhere. Covetousness makes us miserable. Wanting leads us into blind alleys. It is not our longings that are wrong; it is the ways we go about meeting them. We run after things that cannot satisfy (Jeremiah 2:13). We do not think the God who made the universe can supply all our needs.

We need to let our longings lead us back to the only one who can fulfil them.

Read Philippians 4:19 again. Take the risk: take God at his word.

DIANA ARCHER

Get out of jail free

Now we have been released from the law, for we died to it and are no longer captive to its power. Now we can serve God, not in the old way of obeying the letter of the law, but in the new way of living in the Spirit. (NLT)

I can't help feeling rather sorry for the Israelites of old – though I do know that God's ways are not mine. They were handed the ten original, life-giving commandments, but they did not have an awareness of the Spirit of God as we do today. We have at least two incredible advantages over them. Firstly, we don't have to obey the commandments in our own strength. Paul goes as far as to say we have been released from the law anyway – not that this renders the commandments invalid (or the last ten days of study irrelevant); Jesus said he came to fulfil both the law and the prophets. It's simply that all the hard work of justification has been done by Jesus, so we don't have to rely on the law to save us.

Secondly, we have the Holy Spirit of God living inside us to help. We are not trying to live up to the standards of the ten commandments. Rather, we are sticking close to Jesus and letting his Spirit fill us, change us, speak to us, nudge us and give us power beyond ourselves.

When my husband became a Christian, he tried very hard to live like one. Within a year, he was worn out. He couldn't understand why it was so difficult. Then he noticed he wasn't supposed to be doing it all alone, and that God was offering his Spirit way of living instead. Submitting to that, and asking God to fill him and empower him every day, changed everything.

God is so kind! Not only has he rescued us from sin, he has also provided the means to live a remade, reborn, constantly new, empowered life.

Don't even try to live a ten-commandment life without God. It's all about relationship.

DIANA ARCHER

Love over all

'Now I am giving you a new commandment: love each other. Just as I have loved you, you should love each other.' (NLT)

One of my favourite verses in John's Gospel is verse 1 of chapter 13: 'He had loved his disciples during his ministry on earth, and now he loved them to the very end' (NLT). This is followed by Jesus washing his disciples' feet with love and care. It is an amazing picture: the rabbi removing his outer robe to wash his followers' feet – bending down in front of them, serving them and teaching them love in action. Then Jesus reassures Peter that he needs only to have his feet washed, as he is already accepted just as he is.

If Jesus knelt before you and offered to wash your feet, could you receive it? How would you feel? It was what the disciples needed right then. It was an expression of love and humility they never forgot, and one which has been a powerful example to Christians down the centuries.

In Australia some years ago, as the Church helped to lead the way in reconciliation between white and Aborigine, white archbishops knelt and washed the feet of Aboriginal archbishops in a special service. The two crosses of the Anglican Church and the Aboriginal Church were bound together. It was a powerful symbol of intention, and an essentially Jesus-centred act. It demonstrated love.

It's all about love, and the ten commandments are an incredible gift from an all-loving God for our good. He knows us all individually and intimately. He wants a relationship with us more than we can possibly imagine – and that includes you and it includes me. So, as you continue into this new year, forget resolutions and choose instead to enjoy the adventure of doing things God's way.

'Define yourself radically as one beloved by God. This is the true self. Every other identity is illusion' – Brennan Manning, Abba's Child: The cry of the heart for intimate belonging *(Navpress, 2002).*

DIANA ARCHER

Reading the Bible

Tania Vaughan writes:

Reading God's word need not be an obligation or a chore. Yet for many years that is exactly what it felt like for me. The pressure I felt to get my daily reading done meant it became an arduous task to complete and not something I looked forward to. I found it easier to read what others said, and I spent more time reading books about the Bible than the Bible itself. It wasn't until I started writing Bible studies and teaching groups that the Bible really came alive for me.

In preparing for teaching or writing devotions, I come to God's word with an expectation that God will speak and show me something I can share with others. When I started expecting to hear from God through the Bible, he was faithful and spoke through his word. It is still easier to come to God's word with expectation when I am preparing for a teaching session or conference, but I try to incorporate that confidence into my daily readings, knowing I will hear from God if I take the time to listen.

Experiencing God's word in this way ignited in me a hunger for the Bible. I started Bible college in 2015, where I learned to study God's word in a whole new way. I learned the importance of having some understanding of biblical history and cultural context. This doesn't mean you need to read big heavy academic books that make little sense to you, but it does mean being curious about the time and place the Bible books are set. I learned that people who write about the Bible are not always right – and this knowledge raised questions for me, driving me back into the Bible to discover the truth for myself. I wanted to see what God was saying to me, not Bible commentators. The Bible is, above all, the revelation of God. It's your way of getting to know him and building a relationship with him.

My prayer, as you read and study the Bible using these notes, is that you will come with the expectation of hearing from God. My hope is that you will see more of God, and develop a hunger to know him better and deepen your relationship with him. I pray you will see value in God's word and fall in love with scripture as I have.

Asking for directions

Happy are those who do not follow the advice of the wicked, or take the path that sinners tread, or sit in the seat of scoffers. (NRSV)

I was a year into my course at Bible college and struggling with whether or not I should continue into another year. I contacted every friend, spiritual mentor and mature person I could find to talk it through and seek advice. I wanted someone to tell me which way to go. I got lots of good advice but I still wasn't sure. As I continued to seek, one good friend asked me, 'Have you asked God?'

Of course I'd prayed but I hadn't actually asked God what I should do. So I sat down, asked God a simple question and waited. I didn't have to wait long. Within ten minutes of getting on with chores I had my answer. A Bible verse dropped clearly into the quiet of my mind. The answer and advice I needed came directly from scripture. However, that was only possible because in the past I had read my Bible and meditated on God's word. The word was planted deep within me for when I would need it.

To meditate on God's word day and night, as the psalmist encourages us to do, may seem overwhelming, but reading scripture is like continually seeking the wisest advice available for your life.

I don't read the Bible because I have to but because it is full of value. When we delight in God's word and take the time to meditate upon it, we fill ourselves with the most valuable database of direction, not only for ourselves but for others too.

Do you need some direction? Are you struggling with something? Do you just need some advice? Ask God!

TANIA VAUGHAN

Feeding the hunger

He humbled you by letting you hunger, then by feeding you with manna, with which neither you nor your ancestors were acquainted, in order to make you understand that one does not live by bread alone, but by every word that comes from the mouth of the Lord. (NRSV)

I get what my husband calls 'hangry'. When I'm hungry I become irritable and moody. If we go somewhere new on a day trip or on holiday, the first thing we have to do is establish where we will eat. We've learned that it's dangerous to leave this decision until I actually need food! I have found that hunger means it's hard for me to make clear decisions, and I become frustrated and 'hangry'.

In the same way we often wait until we are slap bang in the middle of a new situation, or facing a problem that is leaving us confused and frustrated, before we turn to God. I have often turned to God's word as a last resort instead of it being the first thing in my day. Now I use the same method that stops me getting 'hangry' to prepare for everyday life. I want to seek God first before I face anything in my day. If my mind is on his word then I avoid that feeling of spiralling out of control I often get when a problem or situation hits.

That spiralling-out-of-control feeling is hunger – not hunger for food but for God's nearness. It's hunger for the peace and soul nourishment that come from knowing his word and reassuring promises.

The Israelites are reminded that what they need to survive in the wilderness is the word of God. Every word of scripture is a tasty morsel that satisfies our hunger and stops us from becoming 'hangry' with life.

Lord, thank you that your word is full of reassurance and promises that nourish us.

TANIA VAUGHAN

How to bake a cake

'This book of the law shall not depart out of your mouth; you shall meditate on it day and night, so that you may be careful to act in accordance with all that is written in it. For then you shall make your way prosperous, and then you shall be successful.' (NRSV)

When my husband cooks, he reads and follows the cooking instructions in the recipe. I rarely do, not because I'm an amazing cook, but simply because I cook more often. I have read those instructions many times over many years. I know them and can follow them automatically without needing to read them again. To be able to do this, I had to read and follow them in the first place.

God tells Joshua to be careful to do everything written in the book of the law. What Joshua knew as the law is the whole of the book of Deuteronomy. That's a lot of complicated instructions, so how could he do it? God tells Joshua, 'You shall meditate on it day and night' (v. 8). In Jewish tradition children learn by memorising the Torah, the first five books of the Christian Bible. Joshua had to read the law and learn it, as I did with my recipes, which I memorised not just by reading the words but by carrying out the instructions. If I had read the recipe book but never actually cooked anything I would never really have learned anything. We learn better through actions and doing things for ourselves.

Just reading God's word will not change your life. The recipe God gives Joshua and us for success is 'to act in accordance with all that is written' (v. 8). We can't simply read the book if we want to see the product of that reading; we have to bake the cake.

Don't read God's word today then walk away and forget about it. Take something with you. What can you apply to your life, put into action or meditate on?

TANIA VAUGHAN

Say it again

I will repeat aloud all the laws you have given. (GNT)

I clearly remember as a young child sitting in a classroom with the sing-song voices of 30 children ringing out with the sound of the times table. Every single day we would repeat out loud the times table. I still remember most of it. I also remember my old home telephone number and the words to more 80s songs than I care to admit.

There is something about spoken repetition that helps us remember. In Jesus' time, many Jewish people did not read or write so they learned the Torah, the first five books of the Christian Bible, by listening to it being read out and repeating it. In this way they came to know the words by heart. I can't remember the whole of the times table because I no longer practise it, but if I did it would soon come back because the sounds and words are somewhere in the depths of my memory.

When we continually read, recite and practise God's word, the sounds become part of us and the words are hidden in our hearts. The problem is when we think of it in this way it can seem like and become a chore. I never enjoyed learning my times table, but I was able to teach it to my own child along with the nursery rhymes I had learned. We repeat what we know. Later in life, as I sang over a friend's baby, I realised I was singing familiar psalms to tunes I made up.

Learning God's word is not a chore but a gift. It is not for us to keep but to use and give away.

How about learning some unfamiliar scripture by heart?

TANIA VAUGHAN

Be prepared

Jesus was led up by the Spirit into the wilderness to be tempted by the devil. (NRSV)

The Bible does not record much of Jesus' life before his ministry begins, but we get a glimpse of him as a boy when his parents lose him for four days after the Passover festival, eventually finding him in the temple in Jerusalem (Luke 2:41–52). The next story about him can be found in the passage just before this one in Matthew, in which he is baptised by John at around age 30.

After his baptism Jesus is immediately led into the desert by the Holy Spirit where he is tempted by Satan. I think it is in this story that we can get some insight into what Jesus may have been doing during some of his adolescent and young adult years. To each temptation Satan offers, Jesus replies with 'It is written…' Jesus knew God's word. We can safely assume that during his adolescence and young adulthood he would have learned God's word. His understanding and curiosity are clear from the way he was listening and asking questions in the temple as a boy. It is in the story of his temptation that we can see the benefit of all that studying. Three times in different ways the devil tries to tempt Jesus, and he responds with a word from God. He doesn't just know the word; he puts it to use against the lies of the enemy.

Believers are still tempted by those same lies about identity (v. 3); about whether God keeps his promises (v. 6); and about what we need in our lives (v. 9). When we know God's word we can answer those lies with God's truth.

Write your favourite verse or promise from God on a Post-it note and stick it somewhere that you will see every day as a reminder of the truth.

TANIA VAUGHAN

Are you truly alive?

'Thus says the Lord God to these bones: I will cause breath to enter you, and you shall live.' (NRSV)

I have suffered from depression for many years. At its worst I was hospitalised for my own safety. I was dead inside and I couldn't see how there would ever be a way out. Any hope of normal life was gone. I didn't know God then but I know now that he knew me.

This story reminds me a lot of those bad times. I imagine that God was looking upon me in much the same way as he looks at the dry bones and asks Ezekiel, 'Can these bones live?' (v. 3). God put his breath in me and I did live. He breathed life into my dry bones. How? Just as he does it here. When we read these strange and confusing verses slowly we can see they are not the script of a gruesome movie but an instruction for what gives us life. God tells Ezekiel to tell the bones to 'hear the word of the Lord' (v. 4), so Ezekiel speaks God's words over them. The result is that they assemble and become covered with flesh. Then God tells Ezekiel to prophesy to the breath to enter the bodies, and they live (v. 10). There is power in the word of God.

I found life in the same way one day as I sat and listened to the word of God in church. As I heard the verses of scripture, God breathed life into me and I broke down and gave my life to Jesus.

God gives us his word so that we will know him (v. 6) – not just so we can dutifully absorb passages of scripture, but so we can enter into a relationship with him.

Read the verses again slowly and note in your journal or underline all of the life-giving words.

TANIA VAUGHAN

Seeing is not believing

Jesus told [Thomas], 'Because you have seen me, you have believed; blessed are those who have not seen and yet have believed.' (NIV)

I love writing articles and devotions on my blog, and have become an invested member in a virtual community of bloggers. One of the things we talk about is how to get more people to read what we're writing. It becomes a numbers game to measure the worth of our writing. Like Thomas we need to see and touch something tangible to really believe it. I thought I needed the numbers to give my writing purpose, but my purpose for writing is not to get comments or followers. The purpose is to write what God is saying through me to what could be just one person – not just any person but the one God wants to connect with.

Similarly, John tells us his purpose for writing his book is so we will believe (v. 31). Scripture has a purpose. It is not to be learned out of a sense of guilt or obligation. It is the living word of God given to us so we can know him, and, in doing so, live for him. If we do not spend time in his word, or do so for the wrong reasons, we will miss God's purpose for us.

God doesn't measure the value of our reading by how often we read scripture or how quickly we get through the Bible. We put those pressures on ourselves when we think God is interested in the numbers game. He isn't. He wants us, one at a time, to believe in him and know him. He wants us to have the life Jesus died to give us.

Think about how and why you read God's word. Learn to come expectantly to scripture, to meet with God who purposed this book to give you life.

TANIA VAUGHAN

Letter to the Hebrews (part 1)

Rosemary Green writes:

'The most difficult book in the New Testament, maybe the most perplexing, but the most worthwhile to study and make part of you.' That is my theologian husband's summary of Hebrews! I hope I will do it justice as we think through it together. Be warned: the ten chapters we will read during the next fortnight are not easy! There is general agreement that the author is not Paul (the writing style is unlike his), but no certainty about who did write Hebrews. Barnabas, Apollos, Silas, Philip, Luke and Priscilla, second-generation Christians with high standing in the church, have all been suggested.

But it is agreed that Hebrews was written for a group of Christians who were steeped in Jewish thought, scriptures and practice, and, suffering persecution, were tempted to abandon Jesus and revert to their Jewish roots. The letter must have been written before the destruction of the temple in Jerusalem (which meant the end of the Jewish sacrificial system) in AD70, after a four-year siege by the Roman army. No one knows the location of this group of Jewish Christian believers. Rome is the most favoured, though Antioch, Caesarea, Alexandria, Colossae and Jerusalem have all been suggested.

Understanding something of our faith's Jewish background can help and enrich us, as we see Christianity as both the goal and the supplanter of Judaism, rooted in the Old Testament and yet the final and complete revelation of God to mankind. We see a wonderful picture of Jesus in all his divinity and all his manhood.

We can say the three main themes in the letter are 'better', 'beware' and 'behave'. Better is the dominant one; as the writer pleads for these Christians to stay faithful to Christ and not revert to Judaism, Jesus is shown to be superior in every way: he offers a better sacrifice, a better priesthood and a better covenant; he is better than the prophets, the angels, Moses and Joshua. So beware: don't go back into the old shadow, but move forward in the reality of Christ. Finally the end of the letter has a number of recommendations about how we are to behave as Christians.

Despite the particular focus on Christians of Jewish origin, there is much to excite and challenge us all. But don't expect an easy read!

The supreme Son

In these last days [God] has spoken to us by his Son, whom he appointed heir of all things, and through whom also he made the universe. The Son is the radiance of God's glory and the exact representation of his being, sustaining all things by his powerful word. (NIV)

What a majestic proclamation of the supremacy and divinity of Christ! Pause and read these words again, slowly and prayerfully, and then again. When Philip asked Jesus to 'show us the Father', his reply was simply, 'Anyone who has seen me has seen the Father' (John 14:8, 9). Jesus embodied on earth the character of the Father, but his glory was masked. Only once did the special trio, Peter, James and John, have the privilege of glimpsing the Son of God in all his radiance, when he was transfigured before them: 'His face shone like the sun, and his clothes became as white as the light' (Matthew 17:2).

I find it easy to think of Jesus as the man we read about in the Gospels – a man of purity and power, yes, but stripped of his glory. I find it harder to envisage him as the one worshipped in heaven in unimaginable glory. But when his work on earth was finished, he took his rightful place 'at the right hand of the Majesty in heaven' (v. 3).

So the writer embarks on the theme of 'better': better than the prophets, better than the angels. Jesus not only fulfils and exceeds the Old Testament revelation through the prophets, he is also above the angels. He is the unique Son, whom they worship. They are ministering spirits, sent out to serve; he is Lord. If you, like me, enjoy chasing up cross-references to see which Old Testament verses the writer is quoting, you will find them in Psalm 2:7; 2 Samuel 7:14; Psalm 104:4; Psalm 45:6, 7; Psalm 102:25–27; and Psalm 110:1. (The reference for verse 6 seems obscure, so I have omitted it.) I hope you have read the introductory page in this study guide to help you get the most from this difficult but enriching book.

Use verses 8 and 9 to worship the Son who is 'the radiance of God's glory'.
ROSEMARY GREEN

Fully human

[Jesus] had to be made like [Abraham's descendants], fully human in every way, in order that he might become a merciful and faithful high priest in service to God… Because he himself suffered when he was tempted, he is able to help those who are being tempted. (NIV)

Jesus is the divine Son of God, 'the radiance of God's glory' (1:3). Jesus is hugely superior to the angels. Yet he 'was made lower than the angels for a little while' (v. 9). When he came to earth to be born as a man, Jesus did not lay aside his divine nature, but he did lay aside his divine glory. And he became fully human, identifying with our weaknesses, subject to temptation and suffering. It is a poor comparison, but imagine what it would be like for you or me to become an ant. Why did Jesus do it? So we might be released from the power of the devil and the fear of death.

You might say, 'But I know all this. I know that Jesus is God's Son, born as a baby in the humblest of surroundings; we celebrated Christmas recently.' But do we sometimes feel overfamiliar with, even blasé about, a truth some of us have known for decades? As I write, I find in myself fresh wonder at this utterly amazing truth. Jesus chose to be stripped of his glory to share in our frailty. Pause to dwell on that thought.

My wonder is underlined as I read verse 17. Jesus was the only one who could step in to make atonement for our sin, so that we could be released to share in his eternity. We will think more about this later. In a symbolic act of God's forgiveness on the annual Day of Atonement in the Jewish calendar, the high priest offered sacrifices for his own and the people's sins before sending a live scapegoat into the desert. Jesus, fully divine and fully human, was both high priest and scapegoat, in a sacrifice that needed no repetition.

'Because he himself suffered when he was tempted, he is able to help those who are being tempted' (v. 18). Remember this today whenever you are tempted to stray from God's way for you.

ROSEMARY GREEN

Greater than Moses

Moses was faithful as a servant in all God's house, bearing witness to what would be spoken by God in the future. But Christ is faithful as the Son over God's house. (NIV)

We remember that this letter was addressed to Christians whose Jewish heritage was in their DNA. Now, in a time of persecution, they were tempted to abandon Christ and revert to the faith and practices of their upbringing. The writer does not want to belittle the faith of their parents. He (or she) fully respects it as the foundation of how they were (and we are) to understand Jesus. What went before in the Old Testament was good and necessary, but incomplete. Christ came to fulfil and supersede the old.

Moses was a mighty leader, the saviour who had led the Israelites from slavery in Egypt into Canaan. He was intimate with God: we read in Exodus 33:11 'The Lord would speak to Moses face to face, as one speaks to a friend.' He 'was faithful as a servant in all God's house' (v. 5). But he was still God's servant. Christ was faithful not as a servant but as God's Son.

The original readers were urged to fix their eyes on Jesus, looking forward and upward, not back to Moses. We, too, must fix our eyes on Jesus, who is greater than any other; on Jesus, in whom our confidence rests. What does that mean in practice?

Here's a glimpse of my prayer life one day recently, starting at the bus stop: 'Lord, these buses are erratic. Please don't let me be late for my eye appointment. And if you want me to speak about you in the bus or in the waiting room, help me to be alert and natural.'

Later: 'Lord, thank you for that conversation with the stranger in the waiting room; may it help her one tiny step towards finding you. I praise you for the good report on my eye condition. And thank you for Jenny and Peter giving their time to help me today.'

Lord, I pray that my eyes may be fixed on you today, whatever the day brings.

ROSEMARY GREEN

Beware!

See to it, brothers and sisters, that none of you has a sinful, unbelieving heart that turns away from the living God. But encourage one another daily, as long as it is called 'Today', so that none of you may be hardened by sin's deceitfulness. (NIV)

How easy it is to adopt an 'I'm all right, Jack' attitude. We see how others are failing spiritually but don't want to look in the mirror, or have the spotlight turned on ourselves. Paul wrote in 1 Corinthians 10:12, 'If you think you are standing firm, be careful that you don't fall!'

The writer makes powerful use of Psalm 95:7–8 (a psalm I used to sing regularly, growing up in a traditional Anglican church): 'Today, if you hear his voice, do not harden your hearts' (vv. 7–8). It is emphasised by repetition. The psalm refers to the Israelites' wandering in the wilderness for 40 years after their miraculous escape across the Red Sea from bondage in Egypt. They reached the edge of the promised land in a year. But, in fear and disbelief, the people listened to the discouraging majority report of ten of the spies sent to explore, rather than to the optimistic Caleb and Joshua. They were condemned to another 39 years in the desert and the death of a generation. (If you don't remember the story, read it in Numbers chapters 13 and 14.) They hardened their hearts and they rebelled against Moses and against God. And they were punished for it.

The writer's plea to these Jewish Christians is: 'You have had a miraculous rescue from the bondage of sin through the One who is greater than Moses. Don't harden your hearts now; don't turn back to the old ways; move forward in the "promised land" with Jesus.' The plea to us is the same: 'Don't relapse into a mundane Christian experience.' I've been there. 'Sin's deceitfulness' (v. 13) of resentment, busyness, disobedience and carelessness have all taken me into seasons when I didn't deliberately abandon Christ, but I drifted into pallid Christianity. Wholehearted commitment brings much greater joy.

'Encourage one another daily' (v. 13). We need to help one another stand firm. How can you help your Christian group to grow in love and mutual encouragement? Lord, may I encourage someone else today.

ROSEMARY GREEN

Our future rest

There remains, then, a Sabbath-rest for the people of God; for anyone who enters God's rest also rests from their works, just as God did from his. Let us, therefore, make every effort to enter that rest, so that no one will perish by following their example of disobedience. (NIV)

I was very puzzled at first as I read these verses about rest. Then I saw that the writer is taking a long-term view: 'Keep going faithfully with Christ now, so that in eternity you may enjoy the "Sabbath-rest" that God enjoyed on completing his creation.' Entry into the promised land under Joshua was a temporary goal, a temporary rest (not that they enjoyed much rest in overwhelming the Canaanites!). The long-term goal is the privilege of sharing God's rest in eternity.

I confess my eyes rarely look that far ahead, even as I get older, aware that I have passed my 'fourscore years'. There is still too much to enjoy and do: a loving family, a simple but pleasant home, good friends and many possibilities in ministry. Life now is good, despite the challenges of uncertain health and seeing the turmoil in the world. I share something of Paul's tension in Philippians 1:21–24 over whether to stay on earth or go to be with Christ. But he was far more conscious than I am – and desirous – of the 'better' life with Christ.

I am being honest. This is necessary. As verses 12 and 13 show, God knows all my secrets, and he uses his powerful word to expose my innermost being. I used to want to shrink from God's all-seeing eyes, fearful of his judgement. Now I know I am safe in the Father's love, in his forgiveness, in the total rightness of his judgement. I say that as one whose earthly father died when I was an infant; we do not need to experience the secure love of a good father to discover the reality of our heavenly Father.

Thank you, Father, that I can face you as all-seeing Judge in the confidence of your love and righteousness, with my advocate, Jesus Christ, and that I can enter your heavenly rest.

ROSEMARY GREEN

Compare and contrast

Every high priest is selected from among the people and is appointed to represent the people in matters related to God, to offer gifts and sacrifices for sins. He is able to deal gently with those who are ignorant and are going astray, since he himself is subject to weakness. (NIV)

Do you remember facing exam essay questions that started, 'Compare and contrast…'? You needed both to know the facts and assess them. This is what the writer asks of the Christian Jews: 'Compare and contrast the Levitical high priest with the high priest we have in Jesus.' Both were called by God, one chosen from among men, the other as a Son; both understand human weakness; both know what it is like to be tempted, so both can identify with others who are tempted. The big difference is that the high priest descended from Aaron was himself a sinner, whereas Jesus was sinless. Jesus 'offered up prayers… with fervent cries and tears' (v. 7) in his extreme distress at Gethsemane. So he was strengthened, even perfected, as he came through the test, as he learned obedience in his times of suffering and temptation.

The high priest, offering animal sacrifices for sins, was sacrificing for his own sins as well as those of others. But the sinless Jesus offered himself as a sacrifice for the sins of others, and so 'became the source of eternal salvation for all who obey him' (v. 9). The role of the high priest was a stepping stone to Jesus and his salvation. Are you puzzled by the mention of Melchizedek? Wait a few days to learn more!

Read 4:15–16 again. I am hugely encouraged by Jesus' humanity, particularly when things are difficult. He knew hunger, thirst, life as a refugee and bereavement of father and friend. He was alienated from his family, falsely accused by his enemies, misunderstood and let down – even betrayed – by his friends; on the cross, separation from his heavenly Father was agony. Yes, he knows what the pains and joys of life on earth are like; he identifies with all my challenges and difficulties.

Thank you, Lord, that I can draw near to the throne of grace, knowing that you understand my weakness and confident of the eternal salvation you have won for me.

ROSEMARY GREEN

Grow in maturity

You have become dull of hearing. For though by this time you ought to be teachers, you need someone to teach you again the basic principles of the oracles of God. You need milk, not solid food, for everyone who lives on milk is unskilled in the word of righteousness. (ESV)

How do you feel when someone is disappointed in you? Ashamed? Discouraged? Angry? Determined to do better? The writer is disappointed with the recipients of this letter, and we don't know how they reacted. If these verses make us feel God is disappointed with us, how will we react? Hopefully with determination to change. The writer says they should be growing as Christians, serving as leaders. But their faith is stuck. 'Dull of hearing' (v. 11), needing to be taught again the foundations of their faith, they have regressed from their earlier enthusiasm. They still need to be fed as infants, with 'milk' (v. 12). This happens when we fail to participate in lively worship and fellowship, or we neglect to dig deep in scripture. 'Solid food' (v. 12) is for the mature, 'for those who have their powers of discernment trained by constant practice to distinguish good from evil' (v. 14). That becomes true when we hear reliable Bible teaching and get stuck into Bible study.

The downslide is too easy. Busyness squeezes out regular devotional time. Sometimes (as often happens with me) the time is planned but frittered away by 'just one email before I forget' or another practical job needing urgent attention. My appointment with God should be kept as punctiliously as my medical and social appointments.

Other times we stick to chapters of the Bible we find easy to understand, and ignore the rest. Writing these notes on Hebrews is a good incentive for me! Instead of sticking to a few well-known, 'easy' verses, I have to grapple with the 'meat' of its obscurity – and then try to make it digestible for others. So perhaps it's a matter of 'Do as I say, don't do as I do'! I am enjoying the challenge. What are you learning from this letter so far?

Lord, please forgive me when I am placidly content with my existing knowledge about you or my relationship with you. I want my faith to keep growing in maturity.

ROSEMARY GREEN

Once a Christian, always a Christian?

It is impossible for those who have once been enlightened, who have tasted the heavenly gift, who have shared in the Holy Spirit, who have tasted the goodness of the word of God and the powers of the coming age and who have fallen away, to be brought back to repentance. (NIV)

The verses we read today are probably the most contentious in this difficult letter. Let's start with verses 1–3. Have you ever been part of a group of new believers meeting to lay a foundation for their Christian lives? The topics mentioned here do not immediately look like 'elementary teachings' (v. 1)! But all were part of Jewish belief and practice, and we know this letter was addressed to Christians from a Jewish background. If they had come from paganism there would have been a complete break from the past; but our faith in Christ has its base in all that God has shown of himself in the Old Testament – its base, but not its whole structure.

So we move to verses 4–8. This is not to shake the assurance of safety in Christ. Jesus told his followers 'whoever comes to me I will never drive away' (John 6:37). But there is danger for those who have genuinely experienced new life in Christ, but deliberately choose to revert to their pre-Christian faith and practice. We are talking deliberate choice, not casually drifting away. We might compare it to a person who has climbed a tree and found a solid bough to sit on safely – but then chooses to saw off the branch. Crash! God does not drag back by force the person who insists on walking away from him. If you are worried about your flagging Christianity, you are not in a good place but not in mortal danger. You can turn back in repentance and faith to renewed joy in Christ.

So read verses 9–12 and be encouraged. Keep going in loving service – loving God and loving people. Then we will together inherit all that he has for us in eternity.

Pray for any friends you see flagging in faith. And pray for yourself, for the 'bellows' of God's Spirit to revive the embers and keep your flame burning brightly.

ROSEMARY GREEN

Who was Melchizedek?

Melchizedek was king of Salem and priest of God Most High. He met Abraham… and blessed him, and Abraham gave him a tenth of everything… Without father or mother, without genealogy, without beginning of days or end of life, resembling the Son of God, he remains a priest for ever. (NIV)

I have always been mystified about Melchizedek and have tended to bypass him, leaving him aside as 'too difficult'. Now I begin to see how important he is in the writer's persuasion that Jesus is better than all the Jews had before; in this case he is a better high priest. At first sight it seems strange that so much is made of one about whom there are just five verses in the Old Testament. We meet Melchizedek in Genesis 14:17–20, when Abraham returns from rescuing his nephew Lot after his capture by a coalition of four kings. Melchizedek, whose name means 'king of righteousness', is described as 'king of Salem' (i.e. Jerusalem; *salem* means 'peace') and 'priest of God Most High' (v. 1). He appears from nowhere, 'without genealogy' (v. 3) (normally so important to the Jews). He blesses Abraham, praises God, accepts a tenth of the loot – and then disappears! The only other reference to him is in Psalm 110, a psalm that looks forward to the Messiah. We read in verse 4, 'You [the Messiah] are a priest for ever, in the order of Melchizedek', a phrase quoted repeatedly in Hebrews.

'Just think how great he was' (v. 4). The first strand in the argument about Melchizedek's superiority (and so about Jesus, 'priest for ever, in the order of Melchizedek') is about paying tithes. The priests, descended from Aaron and Levi, collected tithes from their fellow Israelites. The lesser paid tithes to the greater. Abraham paid tithes to Melchizedek, so he must have been greater even than the revered patriarch Abraham – and therefore greater than his descendants, Levi, Aaron and the priests who came after them. This is logical, even if it seems complicated.

Paul says 'all Scripture is God-breathed and is useful…' (2 Timothy 3:16). But it is not all easy. Lord, I pray that your Spirit of truth will help me to understand the harder parts.

ROSEMARY GREEN

A better high priest

Such a high priest truly meets our need – one who is holy, blameless, pure, set apart from sinners, exalted above the heavens. Unlike the other high priests, he does not need to offer sacrifices day after day, first for his own sins, and then for the sins of the people. (NIV)

Our reading today starts with a question: 'If perfection could have been attained through the Levitical priesthood… why was there still need for another priest to come?' (v. 11) We who are far from the priestly system may wonder why the question is necessary; but for those who first read this letter, steeped in the old ways of thinking, it was revolutionary. 'For when the priesthood is changed, the law must be changed also' (v. 12). Understanding this can lead us to a new appreciation of Jesus and what he has done for us.

The new priest is 'in the order of Melchizedek, not in the order of Aaron' (v. 11). That was a shock to the system for these Jews. And Jesus came from the non-priestly tribe of Judah, not Levi – more shockwaves. But the writer is clear in verses 18–19: the old way was weak, useless and imperfect. The new is better by far. The new priesthood, unlike the old, was introduced by God's solemn oath: 'The Lord has sworn and will not change his mind' (v. 21, quoting Psalm 110:4 again). The new priest had no sin, so – unlike the Aaronic priest – no need to sacrifice for his own sins. He sacrificed himself, not animals, as both priest and offering.

The old priests died, so there were many. But Jesus, risen from the dead and ascended, lives for ever; he is the one and only permanent, perfect priest. His sacrifice, unlike the animal sacrifices, is once for all, and needs no repetition.

So what confidence we can have! 'He is able to save completely those who come to God through him' (v. 25). I learned that verse by heart as a new Christian. But how much greater its force now, as I see it in the context of the contrast between old and new high priest.

Thank you, Lord, that I can come to you without any human intermediary. Thank you for the confidence that your death for my sin is complete, perfect and once for all.

ROSEMARY GREEN

A new covenant

'I will put my laws in their minds and write them on their hearts. I will be their God, and they will be my people. No longer will they teach their neighbours, or say to one another, "Know the Lord," because they will all know me.' (NIV)

An exciting new day had dawned – new covenant, new promises, new relationship, new assurance of forgiveness. The old covenant was based on 'If you will, then I will…' (e.g. Exodus 19:5: if you will obey, you will be my special people). The old covenant was a necessary stepping stone to understanding God and his ways, and to relationship with him. It educated but could not redeem. Sinful people could never live up to the standards of a holy God.

But now the day of the new covenant, promised through Jeremiah (31:31–34) six centuries earlier, had arrived. It is not a covenant of law and obedience, the covenant the people of Israel broke. It is a covenant of relationship and inner change. We notice three marks of this new covenant:

1. It is internal, not external (v. 10). His law is in our minds, written in our hearts; that implies to me God's Holy Spirit at work within.
2. It is personal, not collective (v. 11). The old covenant was with the group; the new covenant is with the individual, and calls for personal response. Some individuals, like Abraham, Moses and David, had an intimate friendship with God, but it was not universal.
3. Sin is forgiven, not merely overlooked (v. 12). The Lord wants each of us to have full confidence that he really does forgive sin. 'If we confess our sins, he is faithful and just and will forgive us our sins and purify us from all unrighteousness' (1 John 1:9).

Let us ensure that we enjoy to the full these marks of the new covenant: inner change, personal relationship and assured forgiveness.

Lord, thank you for the immense privileges I have under the new covenant: your power within, close relationship with you and assurance that when I confess my failures you do forgive.

ROSEMARY GREEN

The old and the new

The blood of goats and bulls… sprinkled on those who are ceremonially unclean sanctifies them so that they are outwardly clean. How much more, then, will the blood of Christ, who through the eternal Spirit offered himself unblemished to God, cleanse our consciences from acts that lead to death, so that we may serve the living God! (NIV)

As the writer nears the end of his theological argument (yes, I know it has been heavy going!) he spells out, even more vividly, the contrast between the old and the new. He longs for his readers to be in no doubt at all about the power and completeness of Christ's sacrifice, compared with the sacrifices under the old covenant. He describes the layout of the tabernacle, with its outer room and its inner sanctuary. The priests used the outer room for their daily ministry; the inner room, the Most Holy Place, was entered just once a year, by the high priest alone. But even that sacred time, as the high priest offered a sacrifice for his own sins and for the unintentional sins of the people, was an external ceremony that could not clear the consciences of well-meaning sinners.

What a contrast we have in Christ! Read verses 13–14 again. Jesus did not enter the Most Holy Place in the earthly tabernacle, but the holiest place of all – heaven. We are cleansed not by the blood of animals, which was a token of what was to come, but Christ's own blood. There is no outward ceremonial cleansing, but we have inwardly cleansed consciences. It's stupendous.

I have been a Christian for many decades. I recall my wonder the first time I realised that Jesus' death wasn't just a matter of history two millennia earlier. He died on the cross for me, because I was a mess inside and needed his forgiveness. It was an amazing, humbling revelation that October evening! But over the years it is easy to become so familiar with that huge truth we can be almost blasé about it. I am glad to have my amazement renewed today.

Lord, please help me to grasp a bit more of the enormity of your sacrificial death for me.

ROSEMARY GREEN

Once for all

Day after day every priest stands and performs his religious duties; again and again he offers the same sacrifices, which can never take away sins. But when this priest had offered for all time one sacrifice for sins, he sat down at the right hand of God. (NIV)

Sometimes the writer of Hebrews seems to go round in circles. We wonder, haven't we read this before? But the writer recognises the deep-rootedness of the recipients' old beliefs, and wants to drive home to them that they really have been enriched by following Christ. The regular repetition of priestly sacrifices, with the annual reminder of sins, shows their incompleteness. 'It is impossible for the blood of bulls and goats to take away sins' (v. 4).

The writer seems to love quoting from scripture and now turns to Psalm 40. A thousand years earlier David, the psalmist, saw that the sacrifice of obedience was more pleasing to God than the traditional sacrifice of animals. Jesus came with the same attitude: 'I have come to do your will, my God' (v. 7) It's like his prayer in Gethsemane: 'Not what I will, but what you will' (Mark 14:36).

And so 'this priest' – Jesus – came to offer 'for all time one sacrifice for sins' (v. 12). No longer was there need for 'the same sacrifices repeated endlessly year after year' (v. 1). They were ineffective. They brought no freedom from guilt, just a regular reminder of sin.

By contrast, Jesus' words from the cross, 'It is finished' (John 19:30), speak of triumph; his work on earth was completed. His sacrifice of himself, in obedience to his Father, had atoned for the world's sins. For himself, he earned the right to sit at the right hand of God. For us: 'By one sacrifice he has made perfect for ever those who are being made holy' (v. 14). Indeed, 'sacrifice for sin is no longer necessary' (v. 18). 'Their sins and lawless acts I will remember no more,' says the Holy Spirit (v. 17). And because God's Spirit lives in us we can grasp the truth that we are forgiven. Take that in!

God's indwelling Spirit can help me grasp the truth that I am forgiven. The same Spirit can help me live obediently, sharing Jesus' lifelong motto: 'I do always those things that please him' (John 8:29, KJ21).

ROSEMARY GREEN

Persevere!

Brothers and sisters, since we have confidence to enter the Most Holy Place by the blood of Jesus… and since we have a great priest over the house of God, let us draw near to God… Let us hold unswervingly to the hope we profess. (NIV)

It is no surprise that the author finishes the solid doctrinal section of the letter, in which the supremacy of Christ has been painstakingly demonstrated in every area, by launching into another warning against deserting Christ. With such a high priest, with such a covenant, with such a sacrifice, we can draw near to God 'in full assurance of faith' (v. 22, KJ21).

Under the old covenant only the high priest could enter the Most Holy Place – and that just once a year. The writer refers to the curtain that separated the inner sanctum of the tabernacle (or temple) from the outer room. Matthew tells us that, when Jesus died, that curtain was torn in two from top to bottom, as if by God's hand (Matthew 27:51). Now every Christian believer is free to come to God at any time, with 'our hearts sprinkled to cleanse us from a guilty conscience' (v. 22), in the assurance of being forgiven; and with 'our bodies washed with pure water' (v. 22) – a reference to baptism, when the outward application of water is a visible sign of the inner spiritual cleansing wrought by God.

So let us draw near, let us hold fast to our hope, let us encourage one another in love. Let us go forward, not back from the reality to the shadow. If we do, there is no other sacrifice for sin in reserve, as it were – only the certainty of judgement. The Lord of the Church will judge his people, just as the God of Israel did. After the warning of verses 26–31 the writer turns again to encouragement, reminding the recipients how they endured before in the face of persecution, and pleading for them to persevere in faith.

Lord, thank you for opening my eyes afresh to see how great you are. I pray that I may live, always thrilled with you and determined to move forward with you.

ROSEMARY GREEN

Church as family

Bex Lewis writes:

If we asked non-churchgoers what church meant, they would probably say the building in which people meet together. As Christians we know the theological meaning of church is the whole body of believers. In addition, it often appears that church is seen as a place for people to go, and the wider notion of 'church as family' has somehow become 'church for families'.

Relevant magazine recently described the church as 'a colony of Heaven', heaven being 'the beginning of the world as it was always meant to be'. Therefore the church is expected to be heaven on earth. Church, then, has a much wider purpose than to provide services 'for the family' as it seeks to transform both society and individuals to be more Christlike.

There are some radical notions here that don't fit comfortably with our individualistic 21st-century culture. Church as family is not about blood relations. In its 24/7 form, it's about the places where we meet God, and learning how to meet God everywhere else.

If we think about church as a place to go, it becomes somewhere to escape from the rest of the world, rather than a community (at both the global and local level) where we learn to grow as people of faith, to become more Christlike. With church as family, we learn to lay down our lives in the name of the common good, drawing glory to God and engaging with the places we live in, and the people with whom we live. As we inhabit those spaces, which for me include online as well as physical communities, we are called to step into places of injustice, shine the light of God on them and actively engage with them.

When churches describe themselves as a 'family church', there is a danger that they have settled into the comfort of those they know. It can be all about being nice to each other, with no hard questions asked; but we need to be bolder than that. Within all families, there are relationships that are fractured, broken, confused and complicated. For some, family relationships are hard; for some, a blessing. We need to look to God for a different model: radical ideas of doing life together and making the church family a place of welcome for all.

Adopted as God's children

God had already decided that through Jesus Christ he would make us his children – this was his pleasure and purpose. (GNT)

Becoming a Christian can be likened to being adopted into a new family – a family that already has billions of members! Our name is changed to Christian after the one who came to save us. Jesus Christ died for us; he came because he loved us, and we get to share his glory. When Jesus was on earth he taught his disciples to call God 'our Father in heaven' (Matthew 6:9), and this loving relationship now extends to those adopted into God's family, as we become sons and daughters of God.

I first truly started to understand the challenges and pleasures of adoption when I lived out in Brazil in 1994, working with street kids who'd been abandoned. Regarded as vermin by the authorities, they were in constant danger of death, and they were seeking new families to be part of. Now, being aware of the work of Home for Good, a charity that seeks to provide a home for every child who needs one, and with many friends who have adopted, I see the privileges and responsibilities of creating a whole new functioning family.

Adoption is not necessarily easy. Children bring their experiences with them, often making it difficult to settle as they fear the sort of rejection they've faced in the past. Similarly, we bring our pasts with us into our adoptive church family, and it can be particularly difficult for those who've had a bad experience of their earthly fathers to engage with the notion of God as Father. Like those who have been adopted, we need to be gentle with ourselves, and with others who have joined, seeking help, support and prayer from those around us as we journey forward.

Lord, thank you that you reach out to us and adopt us into your family. Help us to reach out to others, help and receive help.

BEX LEWIS

We all belong to the same family

Jesus, who makes people holy, and the people he makes holy belong to the same family. So Jesus is not ashamed to call them his brothers and sisters. (NIRV)

You have heard the saying, 'You can choose your friends, but not your family.' As we've been placed into this new family, the Church, we gain many new brothers and sisters in Christ. As with our blood families, in the church family we don't get to choose family members, and there are going to be relationships within it that need work, effort, time, discipline and sacrifice. This can be difficult in a society that tells us to leave behind those who make our lives difficult, and surround ourselves only with those who build us up.

I find this a real challenge, as there are definitely people with whom spending extended time is unhelpful (even within Christian circles!), but I am still called to love them. Part of the joy of being in an extended family is that it doesn't have to be our sole responsibility to look after people with difficult behaviour. Getting up and walking away, however, although available, is not always possible, nor is it always desirable.

It's very easy in our age to live within a 'filter bubble', listening only to those whose views chime with or enhance ours; or, as the common mantra suggests, spending time only with those who can give us something in return.

We Christians are called to demonstrate a different way of living, looking out for 'the least of these' (Matthew 25:40). In today's passage God is asked, 'What are human beings that you think about them?' (v. 6). God thought so highly of every one of us that Jesus became human; he joined in our pain and everyday living, and offered us salvation through his suffering and death, so that everyone can be included in this wider family.

Who have you considered 'the least of these', or too difficult to include in your life? How can you look out for them?

BEX LEWIS

One body, different gifts

There is one body, but it has many parts. But all its many parts make up one body. It is the same with Christ. (NIRV)

One of the beauties of our life on earth is that God made each of us unique! We certainly have human nature 'baked in' to us – we're all made in the image of God after all – but within that we've all got different skills, aptitudes and personalities. Some are introverts, some extroverts, some adventurous, some rational, some creative; all are a combination of many different traits and valuable in different ways. As the Bible says, a foot is not an ear, and nor should we expect it to be. Would the body work if we were all an ear? What would happen if the ear was to try to work alone?

Church is the people, the body of Christ, and we are not expected to survive alone. We are encouraged to be part of a local church and community. We need to look out for each other, care for each other and consider that if one part is honoured or suffering, then we all are.

We live in a digital age, however, and this has made the global aspects of church much more visible on a daily basis, allowing us to expose ourselves to a wide range of ideas from our global family, if we choose to. Digital technology offers us many opportunities to connect with those who are not physically with us, for reasons such as geographical distance or disability. We can all include each other in our daily lives, as well as in special occasions and corporate worship. We can learn from, support and encourage each other from every corner of the globe.

How can you engage with those around you, encourage people in their uniqueness and support those who are struggling by using your individual God-given skills?

BEX LEWIS

Share what you own

There were no needy persons among [the believers]. From time to time, those who owned land or houses sold them. They brought the money from the sales. They put it down at the apostles' feet. It was then given out to anyone who needed it. (NIRV)

Since moving to Manchester, I've been faced daily with homelessness, seemingly on every corner. It breaks my heart, but leaves me feeling somewhat hopeless. I remember a story from Sunday school in which a £20 note was shown, then crumpled, trampled, torn and ripped – yet it was still worth £20.

To God, we remain as valuable and precious as when he created us, however abandoned the world sees us as, or we see ourselves as, and in that we should find hope. Today's passage indicates there should be 'no needy persons among' us (v. 34). I love this quote from novelist Charles de Lint: 'I don't want to live in the kind of world where we don't look out for each other. Not just the people that are close to us, but anybody who needs a helping hand. I can't change the way anybody else thinks, or what they choose to do, but I can do my bit.'

I'm never quite sure what to do when faced with poverty on the streets, but I seek to 'do my bit'. I quite often have chocolate bars in my pocket to give to Manchester's homeless; I give away the leftovers from meals; I give money to food banks to help with their running costs. I have to question, however, whether I'm giving out of my excess, or whether there are ways I could have less and give away more.

Decluttering has become a bit of a trend, but it can be helpful in our daily lives. It allows us to give some of our stuff to those who need it, and in no longer trying to store and maintain stuff, we also have more headspace to give to the bigger concerns in life, such as how to help the vulnerable.

Give us your heart for the vulnerable, dear Lord.

BEX LEWIS

Welcome angels

Keep on loving one another as Christians. Remember to welcome strangers in your homes. There were some who did that and welcomed angels without knowing it. (GNT)

The context for this passage is that most Jews hated Christians and would not entertain them. Also there were limited public places offering hospitality, so welcoming fellow Christians into the home was a necessity.

I find these verses very challenging. Although I consider myself quite hospitable and welcoming, I absolutely love living by myself and treasure my headspace. On Facebook recently someone said, 'If you only ever invite your friends round, that's not hospitality, that's entertainment.'

I have friends who inspire me every week because, though they're not massively well off, they fling their doors open to the temporarily homeless, refugees and those who need somewhere to stay in the locality. They aim to provide a family-like environment for people to feel part of: they provide prayer and a listening ear, and, for those who need it, they find food, clothing, longer-term accommodation, furniture and transportation. In return they are treated to the delights of customs and foods from different cultures. It's not risk free, but it's clearly in line with God's will.

The Greek word for 'angels' could here simply mean 'messengers'. We never know when those we host may bring a special message from God. We do not necessarily all have the space or personality to do what my friends do, but we can rethink our attitude to hospitality in light of the concept of 'messy hospitality'. So many of us feel the pressure to put on 'polished hospitality', where everything is perfect, and consequently see less of people than we could do! Jesus was comfortable with honest, messy people, and told Martha to relax when she was weary from all the preparations (Luke 10:38–42). Let's take the opportunity to be real with people in our homes. Who knows what we'll learn in return?

'Eating, and hospitality… [are] communion, and any meal worth attending by yourself is improved by the multiples of those with whom it is shared' – Jesse Browner, The Duchess Who Wouldn't Sit Down *(Bloomsbury, 2003).*

BEX LEWIS

Live together in peace

Look at how good and pleasing it is when families live together as one! (CEB)

When you think of the word 'family', what pictures, characteristics and questions come to mind? Is it the nuclear unit? Does it involve multiple generations? Who brings up any children and how? Which activities do families get involved in? How does the family have fun? How is discipline enacted within the family? What happens in family squabbles and in a family that gets divided? Do members grow closer together, or do misunderstandings break everything apart?

What if we asked the same questions about church? If we are family, then the same issues apply to us.

Are we listening to each other across the generations, allowing room for wisdom and challenges from young and old? Are activities truly inclusive – for people at every stage of life, including those who are single (churches need to look harder at activities for happily single members!) and those who have disabilities, mental or physical? How does the church have fun together? What does discipline in a church fellowship look like? How well do we support each other in everyday living, in prayers and in practice? How does the church deal with disagreements? These are questions each local church needs to face and grapple with.

One of my passions in studying the online environment is considering how we can engage people with grace and love when we disagree. Far too frequently unhelpful behaviours are demonstrated online, with the loudest (and most damaging) voices drowning out others; there are also theological arguments that are not edifying to read. Disagreement is fine, but, in the manner we respond as we join in debates, we Christians need to demonstrate God's loving grace to a conflicted and argumentative world.

'Let us make that one point… that we meet each other always with a smile, especially when it is difficult… Smile at each other, make time for each other in your family' – Mother Teresa, Nobel Lecture (11 December 1979).

BEX LEWIS

Share life with one another

Suppose we walk in the light, just as [God] is in the light. Then we share life with one another. And the blood of Jesus, his Son, makes us pure from all sin. (NIRV)

In walking in the light together, as Christians, we have become family, even if these aren't the people we might have chosen. Because we all share God as Father, we have a responsibility for each other. We live in a society that talks frequently about our rights, but not enough about our responsibilities to ourselves and to each other. How do we demonstrate a different way of living as 'we share life with one another'? How do we demonstrate inclusivity in a world that seeks exclusivity and individuality?

'A Cathedral Welcome', provided by Coventry Cathedral, often does the rounds on Facebook. One line reads, 'We don't care if you're more Christian than the Archbishop of Canterbury, or haven't been to church since Christmas ten years ago.' The whole thing is a deeply inclusive welcome to church.

God, however, did not tell us to invite everyone into church, but to go out and be the church. Spiritually, how do we show the light and joy God gives us, even in tough times? I don't mean be an unrelenting smiler, pretending you're all right. Within the church family you can be real, once trust relationships have been built, and therefore vulnerable. Author Brené Brown describes vulnerability as being 'all in', being engaged without necessarily knowing the outcome. Part of that vulnerability may be accepting and offering help. It's often easy to say, 'I'm praying for you,' but how do we turn that into practical help: visiting the lonely, providing meals to the grieving, babysitting children, helping out with DIY or offering whatever other skills we can (but allowing the right of refusal to those we offer them to)? Go, in your vulnerability, and be church.

'Vulnerability is about sharing our feelings and our experiences with people who have earned the right to hear them. Being vulnerable and open is mutual' – Brené Brown, Daring Greatly *(Portfolio Penguin, 2013).*

BEX LEWIS

Share life together – good and difficult

The believers studied what the apostles taught. They shared their lives together. They ate and prayed together. (NIRV)

If we're continuing our life journeys together, then how do we nurture this and seek to live by godly principles? The early believers 'studied what the apostles taught' (v. 42), and we have this same material available to us in the Bible – in different versions and formats. I have over 100 versions of the Bible available to me on one app, along with five or six paper Bibles. Each is good for different reasons, and one is with me pretty much all the time. I used to run something called The Big Bible Project, in which we were seeking to encourage people to have 'bigger Bible conversations' online.

Over Lent, the project provided daily conversations from church family members from across the denominational spectrum, each responding to notes provided by Tom Wright, Rowan Williams and Stephen Cherry. Material for house groups was built around a meal (food always gets people talking and sharing), and then groups were encouraged to take their discussions online. The online conversations sought to inspire people (from those who'd never seen a Bible before, to those who'd studied it in depth) to share their unique insights and viewpoints, and to understand the various perspectives that Christians can come from. The idea was to get people to read their Bibles in a different way, to challenge each other's comfort zones, to ask honest questions and to hear new interpretations of Bible passages.

The early disciples gave each other what was needed; they were honest and true; they were respected; and they sought to live both the good and difficult parts of life together. Will others say that of us? Whenever someone has a different view from me I think, 'How interesting,' and I want to have a conversation about the journey they took to reach that understanding. I want to share and learn.

Today, who could you pray for and consider how to bless?

BEX LEWIS

Build each other up

Encourage each other and build each other up, just as you are already doing. (NLT)

We're sharing our lives together, and seeking ways to bless each other with kindness. What is one of the biggest kindnesses we can show someone? To encourage them in their journey here on earth, building them up with our words and actions. We live in a culture of complaint, and I hear from vicar friends that sometimes the only feedback they'll get on a sermon is what was wrong with it.

Positive feedback is heartening; I wrote a book called *Raising Children in a Digital Age: Enjoying the best and avoiding the worst* because I wanted to help those working with children to feel empowered. It's amazing the lift and encouragement I feel, accompanied by renewed energy, whenever someone takes the time to say they found it helpful – and sometimes I'll store those comments up for difficult days.

My friends kick-started a lovely idea for my 40th birthday, when I was feeling particularly discouraged about life. A book and pens were provided so everyone who came to the party could write something delightful about why they valued me. This was very uplifting, reminding me 'I am fearfully and wonderfully made' (Psalm 139:14). Could you do that for someone?

Beyond our immediate circle, what form can encouragement of our global church family take? An obvious way is to give financially, especially to organisations that empower those in supported communities. I was privileged to be taken to Uganda with Tearfund a couple of years ago to see how they work with local communities, listening, supporting and encouraging, rather than coming in with a 'we know best' plan. Do pray for them.

Day-to-day living can be challenging. Who can you encourage today? Let them know you are praying for them, and that they are valuable to you, and to God.

BEX LEWIS

Teach and correct each other

Christ's message in all its richness must live in your hearts. Teach and instruct one another with all wisdom. Sing psalms, hymns, and sacred songs; sing to God with thanksgiving in your hearts. (GNT)

Sometimes encouragement is what we need. At other times we need structure, teaching and correction. In the 1972 film *The Godfather*, being part of the family comes with rules, hierarchy, obligations and beliefs. There's a sense that discipline helps keep the house in order, although I'm not sure I want us to match the model of the mafia too closely! However, much of the thinking behind that model will have been based on Catholic notions of family living, so we won't be completely unfamiliar with some aspects. What does it mean, therefore, to be taught and instructed wisely as part of Christ's family?

First and foremost, to be wise in God's eyes we need to develop a proper understanding of Christ's message by immersing ourselves in his word; otherwise what are we basing our 'wisdom' on? (Have you ever considered reading the Bible one chapter a day? It can be done in three-and-a-half years.)

This passage encourages us to base our lives upon 'Christ's message in all its richness' (v. 16), and there's a strong call to meet in a corporate setting for teaching, instruction, singing, worshipping and thanksgiving to God. There will, of course, be different kinds of churches that suit different people. If you're hunting for (or are a member of) a church, remember it's not going to be perfect; it's good to think what you can contribute to it, rather than pick holes in what others are doing. Be thankful for the opportunities we have to meet together, learn together and worship together.

'Don't tune your heart to each other. Tune your heart to Christ, and then we'll be in tune with each other' – Malcolm Duncan.

BEX LEWIS

Love one another

'Let me give you a new command: Love one another. In the same way I loved you, you love one another. This is how everyone will recognize that you are my disciples – when they see the love you have for each other.' (MSG)

It's Valentine's Day. Are you cheering or despairing? This day has been associated with romantic love since the 14th century, and it became the feast day we recognise in the 18th century. If we look back to the likely origins we read of Valentine of Terni, a Christian priest in third-century Italy who was locked up for performing marriages considered treasonable, and then martyred for his faith. He demonstrated deep love, steadfast faith and God-given courage in the face of hostility from the rulers of the day – going far beyond romantic love!

I want us to think like Valentine – beyond romantic love – and consider what radical love for our church family looks like in the face of cultural pressures, including when we disagree with other members, and how that love embraces those who do not yet belong.

Jesus said the words of today's passage to his disciples at the Passover feast during which he also told them he was to be put to death. He told his disciples they were to become witnesses for him, demonstrating what his life and death meant for the world.

As many in our society see church as an irrelevance, we, Jesus' present disciples, may be the only facet of Christ they ever see. One American survey indicated that many see Christians as judgemental, hypocritical and old-fashioned. What will make others want to join God's family? Do they see something different, transformative and inclusive that they want to be part of? How do we demonstrate the love of God to a world that is hurting? Not by selling a message, but by being a church that invites connection; demonstrates compassion, comfort and healing for those in need; and at the same time challenges those in power to serve with justice and love.

Lord of love, teach us to love radically, like you.

BEX LEWIS

Citizens together

Now you Gentiles are no longer strangers and foreigners. You are citizens along with all of God's holy people. You are members of God's family. (NLT)

A citizen is a person who legally belongs to a country, is entitled to its rights and protections, and typically adopts its culture, practices and values. We are citizens of the world temporarily, but citizens of heaven for ever. How do we apply heaven's values to God's community on earth?

When writing my PhD thesis, I drew upon the work of Benedict Anderson, author of *Imagined Communities: Reflections on the origin and spread of nationalism* (Verso, 1983). Anderson observed how people defined themselves as part of communities. As members of God's family, we want to challenge the notion that to be part of a community, we need to be defined by what we are not (*not* foreigners, *not* white, *not* black, *not* poor and so on) and consider what – and who – we live for. The 21st century seems to be defined by labelling others (especially refugees) as foreigners, undeserving of being part of 'our' culture. Other 'foreigners' are the socially, psychologically or economically disadvantaged. As Christians we recognise that God values us all equally, and that we should be reaching out to each other so that no one is left outside the family of God.

The passage today pinpoints the Jews as God's special people, but the Gentiles have now been invited into the family. The church of Christ is inclusive, and every local church should be an inclusive community. This is not necessarily going to be easy as we get to know each other and respond to God's call to work together as a mission team.

I teach my students that there are four stages of teamwork: forming (coming together); storming (early disagreements); 'norming' (conflicts resolved and intimacy increased); and finally performing (all systems go!). God's family are in a permanent community relationship. As we work together, we have to commit to supporting each other through each of the four stages of teamwork, the good times and the bad.

Lord, we pray for patience and a willingness to listen to those we don't understand. Help us to look for what we have in common, and to offer a powerful welcome.

BEX LEWIS

God takes care of his children

Without the help of the Lord it is useless to build a home or to guard a city. It is useless to get up early and stay up late in order to earn a living. God takes care of his own, even while they sleep. (CEV)

We live within a culture where there's a lot of pressure on us to up the hours we work, to achieve more and more and to be self-reliant. I'm a classic example of someone who feels those pressures. We, however, are part of God's family, so we need to think about the purpose we are living and working for. Are we seeking to build our lives to make ourselves comfortable and safe (yes, I'm asking the question of myself as much as of anyone else), or are we considering ourselves part of God's family, seeking to transform the world we live in?

God takes care of his chidren, and as sons and daughters of God, we can share in his work by supporting each other through difficult times and situations. People saying, 'We can't do anything but pray,' have always troubled me. Prayer is important, but sometimes we're the answer to our own prayers. Maybe you remember that joke about a man sat on a roof, surrounded by floods and praying for heavenly intervention. As he drowns and is taken to heaven, he asks why God didn't save him. God says, 'I sent the fire brigade, boats and a helicopter – what more did you want?' That joke seems to have more truth in it than maybe the author realised. We need to think of those around us and consider whether other members of God's family are the answer to our prayers, or whether we are the answer to theirs. God takes care of his own as we take care of each other. With a sense of his bigger purpose for us, and that we are cared for by him, surely then we can, like the psalmist, sleep more easily.

'The purpose of life is not to be happy. It is to be useful, to be honourable, to be compassionate, to have it make some difference that you have lived and lived well' – Ralph Waldo Emerson.

BEX LEWIS

Stir to love

Let us consider how we can stir up one another to love. Let us help one another to do good works. And let us not give up meeting together. Some are in the habit of doing this. Instead, let us encourage one another with words of hope. (NIRV)

To summarise the last fortnight of notes, we've said we need to look to God for his model of being church – developing radical notions of doing life together, making church a place of welcome and transforming our culture. There is no going back once we accept that church is family.

Each of us comes with previous experiences, good and bad, so we seek to understand each other as we deal with the challenges of those we find difficult and learn to appreciate everyone's different gifts and contributions. We do life together; we learn together, challenge each other and build each other up. We look out for each other, and for those society doesn't want to know, as an act of radical love for God's kingdom.

We've been thinking together how we can encourage both society and individuals to become more Christlike. Grace and love are Christlike qualities that can be transformative if we allow them to be.

Today's passage refers to 'meeting together' (v. 25), and we need to think what this means in a digital age that has transformed how we communicate. The church is the body of Christian believers, and we can build each other up at all times and in all spaces, including cyberspace, not just when meeting in a church building or in physical presence. As we do life together, we build relationships, and we have conversations face-to-face and through social media. We adopt every means possible to develop a genuine interest in the welfare of others.

Finally for today, 'Let us encourage one another with words of hope' (v. 25). Too often we start the day expecting things to go wrong. What would happen if we set out expecting today to go well, determined to appreciate the many blessings we have?

'Who said (life) was something to be fixed? What if it were, instead, something rare to be witnessed, to be savoured, and to be appreciated?' – Brian Draper, Less is More: Spirituality for busy lives *(Lion Books, 2012).*

BEX LEWIS

Discipleship

Victoria Byrne writes:

In the notes that follow I've taken discipleship to mean the attitudes and behaviours we develop as followers of Jesus, as we learn to become like him. Some of my words might not be God's priority for you right now; hopefully some are just what the Holy Spirit has been saying to you. I hope you will let God speak into your days with him. A lot of these notes seem to have reassurance as their main message. I make no apologies for that: God has made me an encourager.

One tool I find useful in my discipleship is journalling what I'm learning with God, and what I think he might be saying. It's a great education to review what I've written months later and see what God did next. This has helped me notice his solutions and the way he works. That often leads to a profound sense of thankfulness. We're disciples of a master we cannot physically see, but he is nevertheless intimately involved in our lives.

He loves us just as we are, yet he is always seeking to help us grow. It's good to remember that God chose us for this life of discipleship, that he has a plan to prosper us. We can never mess up so badly that he cannot get us back on the right road, like a good satnav!

Discipleship involves us facing life's challenges in God's ways and with his provision. We have a remarkable resource: the writings of former disciples who have travelled similar roads to us. As we engage with God's word in the coming fortnight, we will consider things they have written that can help us today, because human nature doesn't change, and nor does God. He gives us his constant presence, wisdom, courage and, most importantly, forgiveness, enabling each of us to be free of our past and to grow and mature as believers. The good news is that God sees everything and knows what he's doing. He's already put people and circumstances in our lives that will help us live up to his great expectations.

Amazingly, Jesus promises phenomenal fruit as we follow him. He said, 'Very truly I tell you, whoever believes in me will do the works I have been doing, and they will do even greater things than these, because I am going to the Father' (John 14:12, NIV).

Trust not shame

'No,' said Peter, 'you shall never wash my feet.' Jesus answered, 'Unless I wash you, you have no part with me.' (NIV)

Some people are very disciplined about having 'quiet times' to read the Bible and pray. I find that the best time to pray is during journeys on foot in the course of my day, but it's vulnerable to interruptions, so I worry that I should be doing better.

That could become an object of shame for me, particularly as I write these notes! The thing is, the inkling of shame I feel about this usually prevents me from asking God for his opinion on the matter. I'm more like Peter than I admit. What am I really thinking? Something like, 'Jesus, I am not having disciplined quiet times, so I don't deserve your help; so-and-so is more deserving of your favour because they have an hour's quiet time every morning…' By then, the likelihood of me believing that Jesus wants to care for my 'dirty feet' is incredibly small. And so, effectively, I'm saying, 'You're not going to wash my feet, Lord!'

John shows that Jesus is unfazed by dirt. He wants to stoop to wash it off. Who else is going to do it? I forget that God came to share his holiness with us, not to shame us with it. When I turned to him again today I found not condemnation, but someone who accepts my apology, who suggested I am often too hard on myself, who loves it when I walk and talk with him. He meets my desire to change with his liberating kindness.

We might be tempted to deal with our problems in other ways: to try to ignore them as long as we can; to talk only to friends and not God about them; to comfort ourselves in other ways. We each have our own temptations when it comes to ignoring God.

If Jesus is walking towards us today with a bowl of soapy water, let's not delay meeting him. He is the one who comes to bring 'life in all its fullness' (John 10:10, NCV).

VICTORIA BYRNE

The Lord is my song

'Behold, God, my salvation! I will trust and not be afraid, for the Lord God is my strength and song; yes, He has become my salvation.' (AMP)

I recently heard a talk reminding me that God has plans for me personally, plans for me to prosper and help his kingdom flourish. Being reminded that God has big plans for the world and his kingdom, but has also designed my part in them, fuelled my sense of vision. I felt greater curiosity to know his plans. The next day I remembered that I wanted to be about God's agenda, not drift along with mine. I had been fearful about the day ahead: I was due to meet a new recruit who was enthusiastic, but we hadn't yet connected well. In an honest moment before God, I realised I was nervous about my unstructured morning and didn't trust myself to use the time well.

Thankfully God had put today's verses on my mind, and I pondered them over breakfast. Staring at the green grass through the window, I declared those verses aloud and prayed.

What happened? I found myself enjoying my day. I was more candid than usual with colleagues, so they prayed for me. They gave me good counsel. My new colleague was more collaborative than I'd expected, and the disconnect was dealt with. God also arranged a serendipitous meeting, which made a huge difference.

I came home singing. Only that evening did I notice the connection. God had been my strength and my song. I had submitted the day ahead to him and acknowledged my sense of inadequacy, but also his ability to overcome that, because he is God and he is mighty.

In what ways are you in need of God's strength today? God cares about those things and wants to help.

VICTORIA BYRNE

Engaging in the battle

In love [God] predestined us for adoption to sonship through Jesus Christ, in accordance with his pleasure and will – to the praise of his glorious grace, which he has freely given us in the One he loves. (NIV)

I memorised these verses one summer. Doing this was a powerful experience, and it helped me engage with Paul's train of thought in a wonderful way. If you try the same, watch how Paul is linking one thought to the next. He is bowled over by God's grace, by how much God is for him, for us, not against us. God has done everything possible in his power to set us up for success.

I went to an evening church meeting recently. I arrived feeling stressed and cross. My bad mood seemed inescapable, until our leader started speaking of God's love for his church and how utterly he loves us. I could feel the layers of defensiveness crumbling as I engaged with God; my earlier thoughts of anger towards someone melted away; my fear of not knowing the people there very well became nothing, and we were united in our love for God.

'Undefended' was the word of that day for me. I had thought my problem was external circumstances. Then I thought it was the walls I'd put up against other people. Finally I realised it was the wall I'd put up to God's love.

The thing is, when we truly know we are loved, and that God is right behind us and has prepared good works for us to do, we suddenly find we are more ready to step forward and meet our challenges, remembering that God is with us and will lead us to victory.

That night my new perspective didn't exactly change the challenges facing me in my work at that moment, but I found I was full of an impulse to care more about the people around me, and my difficulties seemed to matter much less.

For further reading: Psalm 91.

VICTORIA BYRNE

Waiting for the dawn

I wait for the Lord, my whole being waits, and in his word I put my hope. I wait for the Lord more than watchmen wait for the morning… Israel, put your hope in the Lord, for with the Lord is unfailing love and with him is full redemption. (NIV)

In my university days I once walked overnight from Bristol to Bath with friends along a lovely footpath. I recall the hardest times were just before dawn when we were tired but there was still no sign of the spreading light. Reading this psalm I was reflecting on how keenly a guard must wait for the shift of the darkness as the sun brings illumination and greater safety to the people and places they are protecting.

As disciples we have to be faithful to God both in seasons of busyness and seasons of waiting. Each season requires different motivations and skills. Are we ready for that thing we are most praying for? What tools will we need when God answers our prayers? What will our keenest prayer requests be then? What could that tell us about how God is preparing us right now?

As I pray God often reminds me that he will do it, as he encourages me to keep going. He knows the times and the seasons. His timing is perfect. Thank goodness he forgives our childish ways and helps us grow in understanding and righteousness.

I haven't done a night hike since university, but I've had different challenges, some of tremendous difficulty, and I can testify that God has been faithful and helped me cope and grow so that I'm able to flourish in the next season.

Disciples are the ones who stay with God through the hard times and get to experience his breakthroughs. So if you are struggling today, keep going, with your attention on the Son, because he knows the end from the beginning, and he will pull you through.

For further reading: Romans 5:3–5.

VICTORIA BYRNE

Lifelong commitment

Simon Peter, Thomas… Nathanael from Cana in Galilee, the sons of Zebedee, and two other disciples were together. 'I'm going out to fish,' Simon Peter told them, and they said, 'We'll go with you.' So they went out and got into the boat, but that night they caught nothing. (NIV)

Sometimes we lose our way. Simon Peter did: he had denied being Jesus' disciple. After the resurrection, he went fishing. Even then, Jesus was on the shore watching him, and he guided the fishermen to an abundant catch.

Even when, like Peter, we've lost our way, Jesus knows exactly where we are and can guide us into fruitfulness, even if it takes time.

Several years after becoming a Christian I was introduced to Jeremiah 29:11: '"For I know the plans I have for you," declares the Lord, "plans to prosper you and not to harm you, plans to give you hope and a future."' It was during a difficult period of my life. That promise kept me going so often; it was a hint that I would be more resilient than I feared in bereavement, career changes and the other challenges of that long-lasting season.

I've had times since then when I've worried that I'm on a wrong path. One summer recently, God settled my mind about this habitual worry: he showed me by several means that he called me a leader, and that I should start calling myself a leader and stop worrying about it.

Discipleship is not a short course. In Bible times it meant living with and serving a master, learning how they lived life not just memorising a few things they said. It's no different for us today: as we commit daily to Jesus, we find he keeps us on the right path in both certain and uncertain times. God is committed to us.

The failure of Simon Peter, then his restoration by a loving and forgiving Jesus, gives me confidence to trust that my sins, mistakes and character flaws are not going to be my undoing. Jesus died to offer us the chance to live beyond our shortcomings.

Jesus is always with us by his Spirit, but what if he turned up in the middle of your day and invited you for lunch? What would you want to talk to him about?

VICTORIA BYRNE

Jesus cares about his disciples

[Jesus] said to Simon, 'Put out into deep water, and let down the nets for a catch.' Simon answered, 'Master, we've worked hard all night and haven't caught anything. But because you say so, I will let down the nets.' When they had done so, they caught such a large number of fish that their nets began to break. (NIV)

Jesus interrupts Simon, who is tired from a hard night's fishing, and calls him back to his boat. Simon has caught nothing, and he sounds disappointed and maybe worried about having no fish to sell.

Jesus asks something of Simon. I wonder if it is an additional imposition on Simon that he has to wait for Jesus to finish teaching the people before going home. Either way, I love that Jesus doesn't let Simon leave empty-handed. Jesus urges him to make one more effort, this time under his guidance, with resounding success.

One summer recently I was helping on a team at a Christian festival, and the schedule meant I didn't have time to get prayer for myself. I'd looked forward to being prayed for, because when a stranger hears from God for me, it reassures me that God really does know what I need. It is like rocket fuel for my faith. I tried not to mind, but by the evening I was venting my frustration (and self-pity) to God. A friend reminded me, 'God is no man's [or woman's] debtor' (from Matthew Henry's commentary on Matthew 20). The next day I was amazed when God set up a 'divine appointment'. I happened to sit beside two of the prophetic prayer team at lunch and they suddenly offered to spend time listening to God for me. When God gave them a really inspiring, relevant message for me it restored my energy and joy.

I know we don't always get instant reward for the things we do for God. But today's passage rings true for me in a special way because I experienced God giving me a treat. I had figuratively pushed the boat out for him and become weary, and he nourished me.

Have you ever noticed God doing something similar for you? If not, ask him to open your 'spiritual eyes' so that you will recognise his treats for you.

VICTORIA BYRNE

Receiving and passing on

'Go and make disciples of all nations, baptising them in the name of the Father and of the Son and of the Holy Spirit, and teaching them to obey everything I have commanded you. And surely I am with you always, to the very end of the age.' (NIV)

Jesus told us not just to introduce people to him, but to teach and disciple them. I lead ministry to older people in our church, and this has made me aware of the way one generation can teach another.

Not long ago, one of our leaders, who is in his nineties, found something fresh in a familiar passage of God's word. As he described the Roman tradition of adult adoption, we understood how God adopts us into his family. It became a vital part of our group's understanding of our identity in Christ.

There is a natural tendency for generations to isolate themselves from each other. We often think people younger than us don't want to know, but I love to hear testimony and insight from those who have spent much longer knowing God than me.

Happily there is mutual blessing: those who have been Jesus' disciples for a long time can offer valuable perspective on a particular experience, and those younger in the Lord can bring a fresh point of view. The teacher and the taught both benefit. It's also true that God teaches each generation fresh insights and we can offer each other different treasures.

Younger people can fear older people's authority and so keep their distance, but in my experience the older and wiser ones find it much easier to acknowledge their mistakes and speak with humility.

Have you noticed God causes us to need one another? Community is very important to him: 'As iron sharpens iron, so a friend sharpens a friend' (Proverbs 27:17, NLT).

Has God put someone in your life who knows what it is to live and learn, and with whom you can share and grow in faith?

VICTORIA BYRNE

Serving the Lord

Jacob's well was there, and Jesus, tired as he was from the journey, sat down by the well. It was about noon. When a Samaritan woman came to draw water, Jesus said to her, 'Will you give me a drink?' (His disciples had gone into the town to buy food.) (NIV)

Not long ago I made a short trip visiting the charity Asha, who do amazing work in Delhi's slums. I had expected to be impressed by the charity's work, shocked by the poverty, excited by the children's resilience and joy, and probably overwhelmed by heat and pollution. I'd hoped to come back with sharpened clarity about my purpose.

In fact I settled back into home life all too easily. Instead of being galvanised into spontaneous acts of charity, I found myself newly obsessed by beauty, colour and design. My visual antennae were so hypersensitive after India, I was tempted to pack it all in and run away to art college!

I suspect my obsession with beauty was an escape from the enormous need I witnessed. I was overwhelmed by the challenges I saw, but Asha weren't. They faced them with enormous faith.

Returning home, I felt all the assumptions I had made about life, including my purpose in the grand scheme, were up for debate – but no amount of witnessing poverty can make my decisions for me. I still have to actively discern God's will for me personally, day by day, and trust I do some good in the world, though much I need to do on a daily basis seems mundane and merely practical.

Disciples in ancient times had to care for their master's practical needs. No doubt in today's passage Jesus' disciples were as tired as he was, but they needed to buy lunch so off they went. I'm encouraged that they did the right thing even though it was mundane. Meanwhile, Jesus is changing someone's life. Sometimes we'll be having the life-changing conversation; sometimes we'll be off 'buying lunch'. In this case, the disciples were oblivious to what a significant conversation Jesus was having until they met him later. Perhaps Jesus needed it that way.

Take a moment to acknowledge the activity of the day(s) ahead of you, and let God show you what he and you will be getting up to. He may just surprise you.

VICTORIA BYRNE

Sitting at Jesus' feet

[Martha] had a sister called Mary, who sat at the Lord's feet listening to what he said. But Martha was distracted by all the preparations… She came to him and asked, 'Lord, don't you care that my sister has left me to do the work by myself? Tell her to help me!' (NIV)

We tend to fixate on the implication here that Martha's hard work is unappreciated, when we know guests need looking after. But Jesus is making an important point: he approves more of what Mary is doing. She's being attentive to Jesus. In verse 41 Luke records Jesus repeating Martha's name, which gives us a sense of the effort he had to make to gain her attention. Martha perhaps had the option of doing her work while listening to Jesus; instead she is giving her attention to jealousy, anxiety and maybe an undue concern about making everything perfect for the visitors, without leaving mental space for what must be a fascinating conversation. Reading this passage, I notice it seems to be the first time Jesus has visited Martha's family – people who would later become his close friends. This occasion, for all Mary knows, may be the only chance she'll ever have for a private audience with Jesus in her home. However, Martha is focused on the food, whereas Jesus is focused on relationship and the spiritual purpose of their time together.

Confession time: I had friends coming over to pray once, and I spent several hours fussing over the food 'so they would feel loved', but no time praying for my friends or our time together.

I know things go better when my motivations are right, when I am busy for the right reasons. I want to be more aware of God in the moment. How simple that sounds, yet how hard to remember. How easily I go about my day, not acknowledging God. I really want to live differently. I think the answer is to start with Jesus and take my cues from him.

Lord, what will help me avoid being distracted from you in the coming day?
VICTORIA BYRNE

Contagious holiness

As Jesus was on his way, the crowds almost crushed him. And a woman was there who had been subject to bleeding for twelve years, but no one could heal her. She came up behind him and touched the edge of his cloak, and immediately her bleeding stopped. (NIV)

A rabbi like Jesus should have avoided being touched by members of the public, because some individuals, including the sick, would have been 'unclean'. Such contact would have required him to be ceremonially cleansed afterwards, which could have meant not carrying out his duties. But Jesus' holiness wasn't tainted by illness – quite the opposite: his purity was stronger. Jesus had a contagious holiness that could be 'caught' by those who came into trusting contact with him.

As disciples, we are learning to 'go and do likewise' (Luke 10:37). I love the truth that, by his Spirit, we each carry God's 'contagious holiness' everywhere we go. God must want us to be unafraid of contact with those who are doing wrong or considered tainted because he has a plan to shine his light into their darkness through us. But first we must catch his contagious holiness. How?

I recently stayed with a friend for a few days. She's creative and funny, easy-going and kind, and a very relaxing person to be around. But I was most struck by her self-discipline. She feeds herself on the word of God regularly. Even though she has to set off early for a long journey to work, she gets up earlier still, to receive her daily input from God.

She didn't need to tell me I could do with being more self-disciplined. Her life challenged me because she makes self-discipline attractive. She does not demand it of everyone else, rather she simply sets a good example. On a daily basis she does her business with God so she is up-to-date in her dealings with him, even if she does have ongoing questions to resolve. Therefore she displays freedom and contagious holiness in how she relates to others. I found her example inspiring.

Father, help me to catch your contagious holiness. Thank you that I'll carry your presence everywhere I go today. Show me how you feel about the people I meet.

VICTORIA BYRNE

Mighty you

The angel of the Lord came and sat down under the oak in Ophrah that belonged to Joash the Abiezrite, where his son Gideon was threshing wheat in a winepress to keep it from the Midianites… He said, 'The Lord is with you, mighty warrior.' (NIV)

God is outside time. He sees us as we are now, and also how we will be when we fulfil all our potential in Christ. In today's passage God's angel calls Gideon 'mighty warrior' (v. 12) even though that day Gideon was hiding from his enemies, processing his crop ineffectively and believing himself to be the least of the least. If we find out how God sees us, we might be happily surprised.

Once I was having a day off at home with no idea what to do with myself, feeling directionless in a season of wondering what God wanted of me. Then I got inspired by listening to a teaching CD by Graham Cooke entitled *Reclaiming God's Intention*, in which he describes how God can see who we will be in the future and treats us like that now. It's up to us to step into that future. That got me seeing myself in a different light. I imagined what God could see the future me doing. I thought of writing and communicating. I imagined how future me would have a blog. I'd been wondering about writing a blog for a while, but suddenly I realised I could do that right away, instead of waiting until I was a different sort of person, one who would write a blog. So I did. Ultimately that led to being asked to write for *Day by Day with God*. The day I saw myself through God's eyes was like God's angel calling Gideon a warrior while he hid from his enemies. I'm so grateful God sees me as I will be once I've grown through my present limitations.

When God looks at you from beyond time, who do you think he sees? Ask him to show you.

VICTORIA BYRNE

Pressing the reset button

I myself am convinced, my brothers and sisters, that you yourselves are full of goodness, filled with knowledge and competent to instruct one another. Yet I have written to you quite boldly on some points to remind you of them again, because of the grace God gave me. (NIV)

It's March! I love a good restart: new shoes, clean sheets, fresh pasture.

One summer recently I heard the artist Charlie Mackesy talk about the way Jesus invites us to come and eat with him, to join him at the table, in a place of intimacy. That talk stayed with me a long time. Mackesy's straightforward presentation of the gospel showed up the way I'd over-complicated it for a season. Simplicity is something he carries beautifully. We all need to press our own reset button now and again.

We do it when we confess and take communion. We take in the raw truth of the cross as we consume an elemental meal and acknowledge the totality of Jesus' sacrifice. Likewise each Christmas and Easter I re-engage more deeply with God's core message to us.

I valued resetting my theology to Mackesy's simple gospel of being accepted by God, and to the reminder of who we are in relation to Jesus. Jesus is the host; we are the guests, each of infinite value to each other. If discipleship is about following Jesus in the long haul, a regular refreshing of our vision is vital, even when we have been living well.

Every part of our Christian life offers opportunities to engage afresh with God's pure heart. Thank God that Paul needed to remind the Romans of some key truths, so we get to read them. The truths of the gospel never get old, but sometimes we need to be like children and hear it anew – so we can press the reset button.

What aspect of the gospel do you find most remarkable?

VICTORIA BYRNE

Pruning bears fruit

Remain in Me, and I [will remain] in you. Just as no branch can bear fruit by itself without remaining in the vine, neither can you [bear fruit, producing evidence of your faith] unless you remain in Me. I am the Vine; you are the branches. (AMP)

Recently I heard someone's account of such Job-like suffering it shook my hope and trust in God. All of us experience or hear of such lives. I felt like wailing, unsure where truth lay. I was fearful as I thought how unpredictable life can be. Focusing on the things I'd heard, I felt angry, anxious and out of my depth.

I searched my mind for truths that would get me on solid ground. The only thing that helped was reaching out to God himself. In tears I declared aloud, 'You are my God, you are my God.' That felt good and he brought me his peace.

If we are disciples, we have a master. We have the privilege of God's presence as he teaches us in his merciful, gentle kindness how to deal with shocks. We have God as our rock, and he always hears us.

God reminded me that Jesus knew about suffering. He acknowledged that we will have trouble in this world, but he wants us to stay nourished and sustained by his truth and character. He calls us to remain in him, attached to him as firmly as branches to the vine. Knowing that Jesus understands suffering but is ultimately in control made all the difference and calmed me down.

God will have the last word. If we, who are so often hard-hearted, are pained by bad events, how much more do they pain God, who sees all the suffering of the world and intervenes as much as people will let him? How he must be troubled seeing his loved ones grieve, suffer innocently and receive hurt.

One day God will finally restore the world he created to one without tears, suffering, death or sickness. He loves us, and he will not let us down.

Are there any painful situations you've been unwilling to talk about with God?

VICTORIA BYRNE

The fountain of life

On the last and greatest day of the festival, Jesus stood and said in a loud voice, 'Let anyone who is thirsty come to me and drink. Whoever believes in me, as Scripture has said, rivers of living water will flow from within them.' By this he meant the Spirit. (NIV)

Imagine the scene in these nine verses and allow God to help you read between the lines.

Jesus shows how the Holy Spirit will quench the spiritual thirst of people we impact. That excites me! When God gets my attention I grow hopeful that he can and will do far more through me than I expect. I love having my eyes lifted above the humdrum to be fixed on a greater vision. God is constantly at work in us.

One way I receive living water is through regularly meeting with fellow Christians to pray for one another. We eat together (although that's not essential – you could simply have a conversation by email or phone), we share what's happening in our lives and we pray, intentionally listening to God for each other. It's the regularity of the commitment that helps, because we become conduits of God's revelation for each other. This builds over time as we see God at work. We can remind our friends of prayer needs met, encourage them in searching for further insight and celebrate breakthroughs together. I treasure those friendships.

I used not to have such friendships. I worked all hours, and I hadn't found a church where people invested in personal relationships. Now I have, and I took the initiative to meet with people who became friends. I wouldn't be without that now. Through those friendships, God speaks to me even when I'm feeling out of sorts. I love Proverbs 25:25: 'Like cold water to a weary soul is good news from a distant land.' A word in due season can be like a drink of refreshing water. Through the Holy Spirit we can access – and offer – a constant supply.

Father, I love that your word says that, because I believe in Jesus, rivers of living water will flow from within me. Help me be all I can be, and may you get all the glory.

VICTORIA BYRNE

Mission: sharing the good news

Esther Kuku writes:

We must share our faith with others. It shouldn't come as a surprise to the people around us that we are Christians. And it definitely shouldn't be a shock. Christ lives in us. Having our hearts anchored in this truth will eradicate a lot of uncertainty regarding the need to live a life that reveals his goodness and grace to others.

There are no rules other than to lean on Jesus and not on our own understanding. We should allow the confidence that comes from a revelation of the power that lives within us to enable us seek relationships with those who need Jesus.

It's not about winning an argument. It's about demonstrating the kindness of God and allowing the Holy Spirit to do the rest. He knows the hearts of people better than we do.

Nothing happens without relationships. We need to step into people's lives and connect with them on whatever level is appropriate. We have more in common with the people we do life with on a daily basis than we think. But until we reach out we will never know this.

We've all been given our own unique story. The trials, tests and triumphs we live through make us relevant and relatable, and provide the experience that enables us to connect with others. You would not be compassionate if your heart had not been hurt or broken, if you had not suffered the loss of a loved one, or if you had not been misunderstood. No hurt is ever wasted. Both our failures and successes are designed to make us useful in God's hands. They are the material we need to compassionately reach the world for Christ.

We live in a world filled with social and economic challenges. Many people are smiling but secretly struggling to cope. Your story is for them. It will allow you to tell Christ's story, and the Gospel of our Lord Jesus offers the solution to every problem mankind faces. 'Therefore go and make disciples' (Matthew 28:19). It will rarely be convenient or comfortable. However, Jesus tells us he will be with us always (Matthew 28:20).

I pray you will allow the gift of salvation you have freely received to be graciously shared, and that through your testimony lives will be transformed.

The beautiful gift

To [the Lord's people] God has chosen to make known among the Gentiles the glorious riches of this mystery, which is Christ in you, the hope of glory. (NIV)

Where is your God located? This verse tells us that he is Christ inside us and the hope of his indwelling is glorious. It's the hope of peace, the hope of a future and the hope of spending eternity with him. Described as a mystery – a secret once hidden that God has chosen to reveal to you and through you and me – it's too beautiful a gift not to share.

I was unprepared for the feelings of isolation following the births of my children. It seemed there was a forfeit to be paid for the gift and blessing of motherhood: a sense of redundancy and separation from areas in my life that had been full of activity previously.

I started to pray. The Holy Spirit led me to make a list of my local play centres. Suddenly I was excited by mission, by contact with women who might be feeling exactly the same as me but didn't have the hope of Christ, who needed to know the riches of his glory that are available through a relationship with him. I was filled with a renewed sense of purpose and the energy to embrace my new season, and I attended groups at the play centres regularly. I listened to mums' stories of juggling motherhood and work life, and I spoke words of encouragement whenever possible.

God wants the riches of his glory to be shared through all his children whatever environment we find ourselves in, whether it's the nursery at drop-off time or the boardroom.

Ask Jesus for confidence to use his truth to transform your communities, and make it your mission to leave people better than you found them.

Pray for God to reveal his promise, hope and character through your life to others.

ESTHER KUKU

Modelling Christ

'By this everyone will know that you are my disciples, if you love one another.' (NIV)

From a hardened criminal to a newborn baby, everybody needs love. Loving one another as Christ loves us seems like the simplest of instructions. However, there will be examples in all our lives of when we have struggled to love others and have lashed out rather than acting graciously.

God gives us a guarantee in verse 35. If we act right, live right and love unconditionally, our lifestyles will make us stand out in a world filled with darkness.

Positive behaviour and a sound attitude, taking time to encourage people and looking for opportunities to do acts of kindness will help draw others to Jesus. If our behaviour is no different from everyone else's then why would people want what we have?

I remember being in South Africa with a work colleague many years ago. We shared a room, and each night she observed me pull out my little pink devotional book and say a prayer before I slept. It was my lifestyle; I wasn't trying to make a statement – I was doing me. Months later she told me she had started going to church and reminded me of that time.

I am so glad my love for Christ touched her without me having to say a word. Jesus can save and heal, but he needs surrendered lives full of love and people who are unashamed to spread the good news.

We need the Holy Spirit's help to be a reflection of Christ by modelling his character and love. Daily Bible study will assist us in this by transforming our hearts as we spend time with Jesus.

Lord Jesus, help us to reflect your nature in our daily lives.

ESTHER KUKU

Pay attention, be compassionate

When Jesus landed and saw a large crowd, he had compassion on them and healed those who were ill. (NIV)

Jesus was always moved by compassion when he saw people's needs. Sharing our faith will mean spending time helping others without asking for anything in return. We are demonstrating that the God who supplies all our needs according to his riches in glory is alive and cares. Let's purpose to always show those around us we care by paying attention to what they say and do.

I remember being pregnant and commuting daily to work. Quite often people would not offer me a seat, not because they didn't care, but because they were not paying attention. Either their heads were buried in their electronic devices or their newspaper was too interesting for them to see the heavily pregnant lady squashed in the corner. A desire to be more mission-minded will require us to be discerning, prayerful and sensitive of our surroundings so we can see need.

My Facebook account connects me with people who love God and people who don't. I see how both sets of people share the detail of their lives, the joy and the pain. Such personal sharing online is because we want people to care. In some cases a 'like' on a Facebook post has become the modern-day social-media equivalent of a hug – except it really isn't a hug; it doesn't do the job of a hug. Compassion works best in the real world, when it touches, reaches out and listens. Even if we don't have the answer, the power of Christ will be working through us and ministering to them.

It will sometimes take courage to be compassionate and reach out to others. But God is always with us when we obey him.

Lord, please give me a discerning heart and opportunities each day to show compassion to those around me.

ESTHER KUKU

My family, my mission

'If serving the Lord seems undesirable to you, then choose for yourselves this day whom you will serve, whether the gods your ancestors served beyond the Euphrates, or the gods of the Amorites, in whose land you are living. But as for me and my household, we will serve the Lord.' (NIV)

The most important mission field we have responsibility for is our 'household' or family relationships, including our church family relationships. As Joshua prepared the children of Israel for the land of Canaan, he was clear that his most important leadership role was ensuring his family lived by their faith in God. If the love of Christ is in operation in our homes and in our church family, we become a light to others. When people see our relationships flourishing, and love and forgiveness overflowing from our homes and churches, they will be intrigued and want to know our secret.

For those of us with children, we must be aware that they are watching our every move – we cannot live double lives. If our faith is not reflected in the way we are at home, our family will be the first to see the hypocrisy. For those of us who don't have our own children, we share responsibility with others for the children in our church family. Children will watch and learn from the adults around them.

Let's take time out to share Christ with our children at home and in the church, in a way that works for them. Let's teach them about true repentance and guide them through the importance of owning consequences when they, or you, make mistakes. Knowing adults also make mistakes will help them to find it easier to acknowledge their own mistakes and ask forgiveness. As they grow older it will help them understand the restorative and redemptive power of the cross. It is vital that our children learn from us that the God we serve is an understanding father..

Let's ask God for wisdom to be a good example to the children in our homes and in our churches.

Lord God, help me to protect and nurture my closest relationships in every way possible.

ESTHER KUKU

Prayer changes things – and people!

The unbelieving husband has been sanctified through his wife, and the unbelieving wife has been sanctified through her believing husband. Otherwise your children would be unclean, but as it is, they are holy. (NIV)

It is very hard for us as Christians when someone very close to us, a husband, a child, a parent, a dear dear friend is not a believer.

Personally, I do not know how tough it is to live in a home with an unbelieving husband or family member. But I do know there is no heart God can't melt, mould and transform.

The apostle Peter told Christian wives to win over their unbelieving husbands 'without words' by behaviour of 'purity and reverence' and 'the unfading beauty of a gentle and quiet spirit' (1 Peter 3:1–2, 4). The same behaviour is needed in all our relationships where we are witnessing to unbelievers. Paul explains in today's verses that an unbelieving spouse is 'sanctified' through relationship with their saved partner (v. 14). If you're someone whose husband is not a believer, trust God that he is set apart for future holiness. If you have someone else very close to you who doesn't share your faith in Jesus, then as you fervently pray for them and persevere in prayer, trust that in time (though it can be a long time), their 'hearts of stone' will turn to 'hearts of flesh.'

My husband was a Muslim for years before we got married. I had no idea in my early years of faith that I was praying for a (future) spouse who was committed to a completely different religion. Yet here we are today, both loving God in his church and family.

Pray for God to help you not to grow weary in witness to those you love who don't yet know Jesus. Ask him for the strength to daily cover you and them in prayer, and for the capacity to adopt a quiet and very patient spirit.

Pray that a Christian friend whose husband is an unbeliever will remain faithful in prayer and one day see him commit his life to Jesus.

ESTHER KUKU

Christian life is not a popularity contest.

I heard the voice of the Lord saying, 'Whom shall I send? And who will go for us?' And I said, 'Here I am. Send me!' (NIV)

'Here I am. Send me!' This is such a passionate cry. When these words are shared from the pulpit we are rarely taught how unpopular a message Isaiah is volunteering for. Essentially, God warns Isaiah that he will tell the people to listen to God, but it will go in one ear and out the other. He will be preaching to a blind, hard-hearted and obstinate bunch. It's at that point I would probably say, 'Here I am, Lord, but sorry, now I have the details, send someone else…'

There have been many times in my life when I have seen someone, hardened to the truth, hurtling towards a bad decision. My heart has often filled with fear over whether to be honest and say, 'That choice will produce bad fruit. It's going to hurt you deeply.' I have ducked the opportunity to tell the hard truth in favour of being popular many times, particularly when my opinion hasn't been asked for. Isaiah's encounter with God is a lesson in obedience. If we are certain God has given us a message to share, we must share it, even if it means we lose the popularity contest. We may lose relationships and fall out of favour as a result of sharing wisdom from God's word with someone. But the fruit that obedience will produce in the end will be a greater blessing.

We need to pray for courage to speak boldly in love, when required, even if this is an unpopular path that doesn't produce immediate results.

Pray for a life that is characterised by obedience to God's word.

ESTHER KUKU

Faithfulness and protection

The Lord had said to Abram, 'Go from your country, your people and your father's household to the land I will show you. I will make you into a great nation, and I will bless you; I will make your name great, and you will be a blessing.' (NIV)

God is always looking for faithful people he can empower to accomplish his purposes on earth. I love that the qualification is simple faithfulness. He calls the seemingly unqualified and then equips them. He is constantly recruiting workers, and he needs more saints to go out to the harvest.

There's nothing at first extraordinary about some of my favourite women in the Bible, but their response to God's calling is. Mary, the virgin mother of Jesus, when visited by an angel and told she would conceive the Son of God, said, 'Let it be to me according to your word' (Luke 1:38, ESV). Ruth the Moabite forsook her own nation to become part of the royal lineage of Jesus Christ. Her famous words to Naomi are the epitome of mission: 'Where you go I will go… Your people shall be my people, and your God my God' (Ruth 1:16, ESV).

Mary's and Ruth's words embody what being a follower of Christ should be. Those who are followers of Christ are disciples, and disciples are to follow Jesus wherever he goes, wherever he takes us. We lay aside our weaknesses and, as we do that, he takes care of the rest and makes his name great through us, growing by his Spirit our reputation as good witnesses and messengers. Faithfulness will attract the power and protection of God when we step into a land we don't know in order to speak his word and be a blessing to others. For some that may mean foreign missions or full-time local ministry. Or it may simply mean witnessing to the people you do life with on a daily basis.

Pray for courage to say, 'Let it be to me according to your word,' as you step out to witness to the Lord's saving grace.

ESTHER KUKU

Nehemiah

Claire Musters writes:

The book of Nehemiah is often referred to when preachers talk about leadership, as it reveals the characteristics God looks for in a leader. While that is certainly true, I believe the qualities Nehemiah exhibits are those God wants us all to cultivate in our lives.

You will discover that I have worked through the book of Nehemiah chronologically, so that together we can see the big picture of the story. I also wanted us to be fully aware that opposition didn't just happen once, but throughout the book, as I feel we can learn a lot from how Nehemiah dealt with it.

This book of the Bible is rich with big themes such as prayer, vision, unity, perseverance, justice, repentance and opposition – so helpful for our own lives today. I hope you are as excited as me to get stuck into it and see what we can learn.

To put the story into context, Nehemiah is set sometime in the fifth century BC. It is the last of the historical Old Testament books. The northern kingdom of Israel was exiled by the Assyrians in 722–721BC. Then, about 150 years before the events in Nehemiah, God allowed the southern kingdom of Judah to be taken into captivity by the Babylonians, because, despite clear warnings from the prophets God sent, such as Jeremiah and Isaiah, Judah had continued to rebel against God.

The temple in Jerusalem had been destroyed at this time (see 2 Kings 25). However, God had not given up on his people – far from it. Fifty years into their captivity, the Persians overthrew the Babylonians and took over as the new world power – as Daniel had prophesied – and slowly, over time, Jews were allowed to return to Jerusalem.

Zerubbabel led the first group of Jews back, with the purpose of rebuilding the altar. That group also started rebuilding the temple foundations, and by 516BC the temple had been restored – exactly 70 years after it was destroyed. The story of Esther unfolds sometime after that.

Then, 40 or so years after the completion of the temple, Ezra led a second group of about 1,500 Jews back to Jerusalem – and 13 years after that we come to Nehemiah, who was to have a pivotal role in God's plans for rebuilding both the city's walls and his people…

Broken

When I heard [what had happened in Jerusalem], I sat down and wept. For some days I mourned and fasted and prayed before the God of heaven. (NIV)

Nehemiah had grown up within Persian culture, so it is a testament to his integrity and character that he rose up through the ranks to become the king's cupbearer.

He was in a privileged position, and could have felt detached from Jerusalem, but he was keen to find out news. When he hears the sad state of affairs he mourns, fasts, then turns to prayer.

What provocation! He was around 800 miles from Jerusalem, and it was at least 150 years since Jerusalem had had an effective wall so this wasn't a new problem. However, Nehemiah still cared.

It is easy for us to live in our own little bubbles, not noticing what is going on around us, let alone hundreds of miles away. However, God calls us to model his grace, to bring hope and justice for oppressed communities far and near.

In our time of instant communication we are so bombarded by world problems that we can become numbed and detached. Are we sometimes even judgemental? Nehemiah could have labelled the remnant in Jerusalem as lazy; instead, he allows his heart to be broken for them.

Recently God has been encouraging me to hold my days more lightly. One Monday morning, I felt prompted to invite a school mum out for coffee. Monday is normally allocated an admin day as my husband takes the kids to school, but this Monday I headed to the cafe – then discovered the mum had invited some others too. My heart sank, as I had hoped to chat to her about what she had been going through. However, I ended up sitting next to her, and we shared – and cried – and the other mums joined in too. I was able to empathise with not just one but a whole group of school mums.

Spend some time reflecting on Nehemiah's example, and then think about how you react to the needs you see around you. Ask God to break your heart for the things he wants you to respond to.

CLAIRE MUSTERS

Heartfelt prayer

'Let your ear be attentive and your eyes open to hear the prayer your servant is praying before you day and night for your servants, the people of Israel.' (NIV)

God reminded our church recently that he wants to remove our hearts of stone and give us hearts of flesh (see Ezekiel 36:26). Nehemiah teaches me a lot about having a softened heart that is broken and open to God.

Once he had spent 'some days' (v. 4) mourning and fasting he turned to prayer. I think it is important to note that he took time; very often we want instant fixes. We also see here, and throughout the book, that Nehemiah's default position was to turn to prayer. In this, the first prayer we read, he gives us a great pattern for effective prayer: heartfelt praise, repentance, specific requests and persistence. Have you given up on any of these?

Nehemiah starts by acknowledging God's greatness. Then he gives a lot of space over to the confession of sin – even identifying himself with the sins of the nation. He says 'we' not 'they', which reveals a felt unity.

Do we live lives that reflect the fact that what we do as Christians affects us all, not just us as individuals? It can be hard to change our mindsets when we live in such a 'me-centred' society, but that is how we are to live – in full unity, always thinking of others before ourselves (Philippians 2:1–11).

In verses 5, 8 and 9 we see Nehemiah knows enough about God's character and promises to have the faith to pray with confidence. At the end of his prayer, he also shows he cares enough to offer himself up as the solution. There is obviously a God-ordained idea forming in his mind as he prays for its success. So often we can pray for situations but not get involved personally. Do remember we can be the answer to our own prayers.

Spend some time reflecting on whether there are any elements of prayer you have given up on (such as repentance, persistence or thanksgiving).

CLAIRE MUSTERS

The big ask

I prayed to the God of heaven, and I answered the king, 'If it pleases the king and if your servant has found favour in his sight, let him send me to the city in Judah where my ancestors are buried so that I can rebuild it.' (NIV)

The fact the king notices Nehemiah is not himself shows they had a close relationship. Nehemiah is scared when Artaxerxes questions him because it was dangerous to show sorrow before the king: he could execute anyone who displeased him.

Nehemiah then does something I think could revolutionise our own lives if we learned to do the same: he prays to God even though he is right in front of the most influential, powerful person in the land. This reminds me that God wants us to involve him in our everyday lives, and that he can advise us on what words to speak even in situations of high pressure. Is that something you take the time to do, perhaps in a board meeting, in front of a client or when faced by difficult neighbours?

Nehemiah had learned that prayer allows us to hear God's heartbeat and understand his will. This gave him the courage to speak up, relying on God to turn the king's favour towards him. Often I know I fear the people in front of me more than God.

When Nehemiah answers the king, he already has a plan in place. But it isn't his own. He might have been tempted to write a business plan that flattered the king; however, with God's prompting he had thought through the details. He isn't afraid to ask the king for help with specifics. Sometimes God answers our prayers when we ask those most able to help us – but we have to overcome fear and pride in order to do that.

Nehemiah's actions begin to stir up those who will become enemies. This is often an inevitable result of walking with God, so we shouldn't be surprised when it happens.

Lord, teach me to involve you in every part of my day – and to have the courage to rely first and foremost on you rather than trying to curry favour from others through my own effort. I trust you.

CLAIRE MUSTERS

Wise preparation

I set out during the night with a few others. I had not told anyone what my God had put in my heart to do for Jerusalem. (NIV)

When Nehemiah arrives in Jerusalem, he doesn't do what I would expect him to. With the king's approval, he could have announced himself with great ceremony and ordered the people around. Instead, he travels quietly and takes time to investigate in order to finalise his plan. This means he doesn't have lots of people telling him what he should do, and he can listen to God. He looks around and, rather than becoming despondent about the state of the walls, chooses to trust God and respond with hope and faith.

I know I can rush ahead once I have had the inkling of an idea from God; my own head brims over with ways of outworking it, so sometimes I run ahead of him. I also have a mouth that can speak without me thinking about it, trying to convince people I'm right. So I am struck by the wisdom of Nehemiah's understated leadership. He knows you can't lead others where you haven't been, so he takes the time to go there first and then inspires those he will be asking to do the work. He is able to win people over because he is prepared – as well as being willing to build their faith by sharing his own testimony. As a stranger to those around him, he could have bragged about his own credentials, but no – he points them to God. I find that a real challenge. Am I willing to share how God has worked in my life, and do it in a way that points those listening towards God rather than myself?

When Sanballat, Tobiah and Geshem ridicule Nehemiah, his comment back reveals his assurance to be steadfast in God. I long for mine to be the same when I am faced with those who mock me.

Lord, help me not to rush ahead with my own ideas, but to wait for your leading. And help me to stay as steadfast as Nehemiah, even if I am mocked by those around me.

CLAIRE MUSTERS

Playing our part

Shallum son of Hallohesh, ruler of a half-district of Jerusalem, repaired the next section [of wall] with the help of his daughters. (NIV)

Today's reading is full of names that don't mean much to us. But their inclusion reveals God's heart for the individual – he cares about each one and is delighted they are playing their part. Like the credits at the end of a film, this shows how important each person's role in building the wall is.

The task Nehemiah has given them is epic. It will take huge effort to repair the 45 sections of wall, so each person listed has a team behind them. There is real wisdom behind Nehemiah's plans: he gets people to repair the part of the wall nearest their own home. This means they are motivated to do the work, won't have to waste time travelling to another part of the wall, will be willing to defend the area if attacked, and can also involve their whole family (our displayed verse mentions Shallum's daughters were helping him).

Everyone gets involved – rulers, priests, perfume-makers and goldsmiths – apart from those nobles who, we are told in verse 5, feel they are above the work. Are we ever like that? Most of us have an opinion on what needs doing, and can also be quick to judge who should do it – but what about us? As a church pastor, my husband gets a lot of emails from people suggesting new ideas. If he thinks any have merit, he often replies, 'Great – feel free to get started!'

Obviously we all have different capacities and amounts of available time, but I think this passage reminds us we can all still contribute. It is through serving that relationships are built. When we work together, we get to really know others and be known ourselves.

I love that you knew everyone involved in building the wall, Lord – and you still notice what we do today. Help me to be willing to serve wherever you want me to today.

CLAIRE MUSTERS

Conflict is inevitable

[Our enemies] all plotted together to come and fight against Jerusalem and stir up trouble against it. But we prayed to our God and posted a guard day and night to meet this threat. (NIV)

Have you ever started working on something you felt God told you to do, met with opposition and given up, despondent that you must have heard God wrong? If so, you are not alone. But we need to learn that we have an enemy who does not want us to build God's kingdom – and he will use whatever tactics he can to knock us out. I feel this part of Nehemiah's story is vital for us.

Nehemiah has made his plan of action and mobilised the city; they have started building, knowing God is with them – and then Sanballat and Tobiah heighten their opposition.

Nehemiah doesn't allow this to stop them. Life is tough, and we need to be real about that. Nehemiah is very open about this (v. 4), but look what he does in response. He turns to prayer again and then back to building the wall with even more vigour.

We shouldn't be surprised when we hit opposition. Jesus himself says, 'In this world you will have trouble.' Thankfully he goes on to say, 'But take heart! I have overcome the world' (John 16:33).

Nehemiah knows the people's enemies will attack the weakest spots, so concentrates on building those up. Their enemies don't give up – they start to plan their attack, so Nehemiah positions guards.

It is interesting to see how the people respond. They work hard but begin to get discouraged and tired. We shouldn't underestimate the power of words to pull us down – nor the power of God's word to strengthen our weary souls.

Nehemiah encourages the people by reminding them to look to God. Even once their enemies give up, he teaches the people to share equally the responsibility of guarding and building up the wall. What a great blueprint!

Lord, help me to recognise the enemy's tactics and strengthen the weak areas in my life. Help me to look to you in faith at all times. Today I choose to focus on the truth found in your word.

CLAIRE MUSTERS

God's heart for the poor

[The governers'] assistants also lorded it over the people. But out of reverence for God I did not act like that. Instead, I devoted myself to the work on this wall. (NIV)

Here we read about how some of the Jewish people were struggling to feed their families – and the wealthier nobles and officials were charging them interest. As soon as Nehemiah hears about this, he becomes angry. Is this a right response? Yes! An emotional reaction born out of God's righteous anger reveals his compassion. Sanballat's anger in the previous chapter (4:1) was because he didn't like what the Jews were doing, and it resulted in him plotting violence; Nehemiah's is because he has heard about an injustice.

What makes you angry? Does your anger flow out of a heart for the poor or is it based on self-interest, as Sanballat's was?

Nehemiah's anger fuels him to speak up. He isn't afraid to challenge those in the wrong, and neither should we be. What he says is simply the overflow of his heart. As Jesus explains, 'The things that come out of a person's mouth come from the heart' (Matthew 15:18). What is in your heart today?

It can be sobering to ask God to reveal to us the state of our hearts, but it is vital if we are to do as he commands throughout the Bible. 'Speak up for those who cannot speak for themselves, for the rights of all who are destitute. Speak up and judge fairly; defend the rights of the poor and needy' (Proverbs 31:8–9). Nehemiah certainly does this. His words turn into actions, and he also ensures he isn't adding to the people's burden in any way.

There are many things that can block the flow of God's compassion: hurt; unforgiveness; a clash of our agenda with his; fear; lack of time; a judgemental attitude. Pray for an increase of God's compassion in your heart.

Lord, I still my heart and ask you to show me what is blocking the flow of your compassion. I want to reach out to people with your love; I humble myself before you afresh.

CLAIRE MUSTERS

Dealing with criticism

[Our enemies] were all trying to frighten us, thinking, 'Their hands will get too weak for the work, and it will not be completed.' But I prayed, 'Now strengthen my hands.' (NIV)

We have seen how the attempts of Nehemiah's enemies to halt the building of the wall intensified over time. As it nears completion, they begin to get desperate – and things get personal. After trying, unsuccessfully, to lure Nehemiah away from Jerusalem, they begin to attack his character through rumours, deceit and false reports, even getting those he trusts to join in. Rather than praying for God's deliverance, Nehemiah prays for strength and uses wisdom to weigh up the messages sent to him.

I wonder how we respond to criticism – particularly from another Christian. It hurts doesn't it? I can remember, in the week leading up to a women's event I had organised, how the enemy attacked my character in a big way – and used another Christian to cut me to the quick. That person spoke something over me that felt like a dagger being thrust into my heart. I had to take time to process what they had said and ask God to show me if there was any truth in it, and if I needed to take any action. I then had to forgive, and let go of the hurt. Ultimately, God showed me it wasn't a truth and I should not be taking it on board; instead I was to refute it completely in my heart, as it was their issue not mine. It wasn't easy to do, but it opened my eyes to how alert we need to be to the devil's tactics – and how much we need to ask God for wisdom and discernment in our everyday lives.

After so much attack on Nehemiah's character, it is great to read that 'the wall was completed... in fifty-two days' (v. 15) and that his enemies recognised it as a work of God.

Think about your own response to criticism: do you ask God to take you out of the situation that caused it, or do you ask for his strength and wisdom, as Nehemiah did?

CLAIRE MUSTERS

God of detail

After the wall had been rebuilt and I had set the doors in place, the gatekeepers, the musicians and the Levites were appointed. (NIV)

We see here that the completion of the wall certainly isn't the end of the story. God has it on his heart to restore more than just the walls – he wants to restore the people too.

Nehemiah sets about purposefully appointing key people to strategic roles to encourage the growth of the city, which is standing fairly empty at this time. He finds a genealogical record of the people who returned first to help people claim their right bit of land (please do read the rest of the list of names if you have time). Through the practicalities of what Nehemiah was led to do, we can see that God is interested in the smallest of details. What reassurance!

Nehemiah establishes security not just through walls and gates but through people and leadership structures. In fact, everyone has a role. Nehemiah calls residents to guard the parts of the wall nearest their homes. Do we cut and run after finishing something God calls us to, or do we stick around to protect it and ensure it bears fruit?

God was doing deep work in the people, teaching them not to put their trust in a big wall, but in the bigger God who had helped them build that wall. While the wall was the answer to a very practical need, through it they had seen God's protection and answers to prayers. They were now literally surrounded by evidence of God's enabling. They had also seen Nehemiah model how to live in step with God.

On top of all that, the work had brought people together: those who had been scattered in the surrounding villages now gathered as one. That is one of the great side effects of working with other Christians – it builds unity.

Thank you, Lord, that you love detail and also delight in your children working together for you. Help me to see the opportunities you set before me today.

CLAIRE MUSTERS

The power of the word

Nehemiah said, 'Go and enjoy choice food and sweet drinks, and send some to those who have nothing prepared. This day is holy to our Lord. Do not grieve, for the joy of the Lord is your strength.' (NIV)

God's word is key to the people's spiritual restoration. The reason they were taken into captivity in the first place was their rejection of God's law. But here, the first thing to happen as the people gather is Ezra reading from the book of the law. Interestingly, the people ask for it to be read. Many of them would never have encountered it before (owing to being in captivity). Now, hour after hour, they listen to God's word. There is such a longing for it.

Today in the West the average Christian household owns three Bibles, yet a recent LifeWay survey discovered 80 per cent of Christians don't read their Bible regularly. Where is our hunger?

This chapter is the first time we see a heartfelt response from the people. God moves in their hearts as they begin to understand not just his holiness and awesomeness but also his incredible grace and love. They are starting to understand who they were called to be as a people. It all boils down to a question of identity – knowing who God is and who we are in him.

Ezra and Nehemiah tell the people to stop mourning, because it is a holy, joyful day. While it is honouring to God to recognise and confess our sins, it is also right to celebrate that he has provided for our salvation.

When the people discover details about the feast of tabernacles, during which people lived in temporary shelters made of branches, they respond by doing the same. It is a reminder of their rescue from Egypt, their time in the wilderness and God's protection.

It's important to think about where we have come from, what God has done for us and where God is leading us now.

When did you last think about how God delights in you? You may like to meditate on Zephaniah 3:17. Perhaps you have never looked back over what God has done in your life. Spend time doing that today.

CLAIRE MUSTERS

Repentance

Those of Israelite descent… stood where they were and read from the Book of the Law of the Lord their God for a quarter of the day, and spent another quarter in confession and in worshipping the Lord their God. (NIV)

Another key to the people's spiritual renewal is corporate repentance. They use public signs of sorrow and penitence (v. 1).

Their corporate prayer begins with exalting God for who he is. They then recite the history of Israel – reminding themselves how God was faithful while his people cyclically dishonoured him. Like Nehemiah before them, they own their ancestors' sins by humbling themselves and acknowledging that where they are at now is a result of corporate sin. They then cry out to God for his mercy.

We discussed corporate repentance (and the lack of it in today's church) in our small group recently. God made repentance very real and personal to me one Sunday, when I found myself publicly repenting over a microphone at church while inviting the congregation to make the prayer theirs too – or join in with their own. Why? Because I was totally overwhelmed by the cross once again; totally convinced of the central part our own repentance plays in God moving in power in our lives, and us being able to experience more of his presence. Why am I sharing this? Certainly not to boast – the almost involuntary action came from a sudden, immense realisation of the tarnished state of my own heart. I am not proud of what I saw. But I am convinced of our need for continued repentance, and also worried that the concept of repentance isn't preached so much any more. I was recently involved in a discussion about how some churches have liturgies of repentance in services, but many don't as much as mention the word. Whichever denomination we are part of, do we make repentance an active part of our lives? We are told in 1 John 1:9 that it is key to our becoming righteous.

I am so sorry, Lord, for when I become blasé about your faithfulness, and when I ignore the need to keep short accounts with you. Help me to learn to humble myself and confess my continued need of your cleansing.

CLAIRE MUSTERS

Set apart

'The rest of the people… now join their fellow Israelites the nobles, and bind themselves with a curse and an oath to follow the Law of God given through Moses the servant of God and to obey carefully all the commands, regulations and decrees of the Lord our Lord.' (NIV)

In an act of unity, all 'who are able to understand' (v. 28) what they are doing take a solemn oath together after their act of corporate repentance. This oath, or covenant, includes promising to set themselves apart as God's holy people; to observe the Sabbath day, and year; and to give to the temple in various ways.

What they are actually doing is setting out practical ways to show God they mean business. Each of these things ensures that the original covenant God made with his people back at Mount Sinai (see Deuteronomy 8) is restored. It shows that the people have knowledge of the law of God, and that they are willing to submit to it fully once again.

While we no longer live under this law, but under the grace won for us by Jesus, there are still many principles we can apply from this chapter to our own lives. We may find the call not to marry 'peoples around us' (v. 30) quite extreme, yet God knew how doing so would entice his people towards worshipping idols (this was one of the main things that tripped them up again and again).

While we may not live under such restrictions, we are still called to be set apart and, while our righteousness is a free gift from our Saviour, there are still things he expects from us. Our faith in him should not be limited to Sunday services but should affect every part of our lives – our relationships, our money and how we spend our time. Jesus said, 'Where your treasure is, there your heart will be also' (Matthew 6:21). What has gripped your heart? Does God have the number-one place there, or are you distracted by other things?

Spend some time prayerfully considering how 'set apart' your life is – and whether the way you manage your relationships, money and time reflects the fact that you are a follower of Jesus.

CLAIRE MUSTERS

Worship is our dedication

At the dedication of the wall of Jerusalem, the Levites were sought out from where they lived and were brought to Jerusalem to celebrate joyfully the dedication with songs of thanksgiving. (NIV)

It is only due to space limitations that I have left out chapter 11 and the first part of 12. They are wonderful listings of people, showing how God is interested in every individual.

In today's passage we come to the dedication of the completed wall. We see Nehemiah's careful planning once again – and his faithfulness to the important role worship had been given by David when he organised the priests and Levites, and even the songs they sang (see 1 Chronicles 24:7–19; 19:26–27). Whereas Nehemiah had previously stationed guards and workers on the wall, he now deploys the Levites and other musicians to lead the way with songs of thanksgiving; leaders and choirs proceed to the temple – probably along the top of the wall.

Their rejoicing 'could be heard far away' (v. 43). The act of walking on top of the wall is a testimony to the nations around them that God has done the work. Despite their enemies' taunts that the wall would be so weak a fox would be able to knock it down (see 4:3), here they are marching on it! Walking on the wall also symbolises their stepping out in faith to claim it as their own. Elsewhere in the Old Testament we see that walking on a piece of land was a way of claiming it (see Genesis 13:17; Joshua 1:3).

This is an amazing description of public celebration, worship and offerings as the Israelites dedicate themselves to God. Worship is a way that we can dedicate ourselves to God every day. Regularly offering ourselves to him through acts of thanksgiving and surrender not only feeds and nourishes our souls, but also testifies to those around us that we belong to God.

How can daily worship be an act of dedication to God for you? Think about new ways to worship him today.

CLAIRE MUSTERS

Do not compromise!

I learned about the evil thing Eliashib had done… I was greatly displeased and threw all Tobiah's household goods out of the room. I gave orders to purify the rooms. (NIV)

Nehemiah's mission has been accomplished: the wall is complete and so is the transformation of the people – or is it? After such a great picture of worship yesterday, it seems a shame that chapter 13 is in the Bible! Yet, rather than glossing over the difficult bits, scripture shows us people's failure as well as their success.

We were told in chapter 5 that Nehemiah was in Jerusalem for twelve years (5:14), but now he has gone back to Susa. At some point he asks the king for permission to go back to Jerusalem, where he discovers the people have forgotten their covenant: they are intermarrying, ignoring the Sabbath and not giving offerings.

On the surface, perhaps, things look okay – Eliashib the high priest is still working in the temple, after all – but then we read that he was allowing Tobiah (the one who had insulted and tried to trick Nehemiah) to take up residence there.

I am sure the people's U-turn didn't happen overnight; it's always a subtle process that starts with compromise. On the outside we can seem to have it all together – but behind the mask we can allow things to slip a bit.

Nehemiah was radical in his response – as we should be. We are the temple of God (1 Corinthians 6:19–20; 1 Peter 2:5). Our lives are meant to reflect the glory of God, so we need to check regularly whether we have opened the door to any ungodly influences. It doesn't take long for something we wouldn't even consider to become something we tolerate – and then the thing we tolerate becomes something we make room for.

While this final chapter makes for uncomfortable reading, it acts as a warning and gives us insight into human nature. We need our Saviour's help!

Take some time to consider what you allow into your heart and mind through what you watch, read and think about. Repent before God as necessary and ask him to help you live in a way that reveals his glory.

CLAIRE MUSTERS

Easter people

Cathy Madavan writes:

After my ancient mobile phone finally died a slow digital death, I gave in and bought myself a groovy new one. Once I had recovered from the cost, I began to explore its many and varied features beyond the sending and receiving of calls and texts (so old school!). I got most excited about the camera and the various filters and editing options that were now available to me. I could merrily zoom in and pull out and see the world through a whole new lens.

As we lead up to and then move past Easter in these two weeks of notes, we will visit passages of scripture that tell the phenomenal story that lies at the heart of our Christian faith. But it is my hope that we will use a new lens or two in order to survey these very familiar scenes.

Of course we will want to zoom in and focus on Jesus, who is at the centre of the unfolding plot and the cornerstone of our faith. But there is also the opportunity to zoom out a little, as each day is angled towards a person or people who were present at that point in the story. Through their eyes we might see something new or different, as if we are experiencing a new filter or perspective on the Easter events.

More than that, however, it is my hope and prayer that we will intentionally pull the view back even further into panorama mode, and see ourselves in the picture. It's not about taking selfies, but more about seeing how we too are part of this incredible life-changing journey that Jesus took with his followers. When we look carefully, we realise we are in the landscape and that our attitudes and questions are reflected in those we read about. The question is, as the question always was, 'How will we respond to Jesus?'

Let's pray that God will open our spiritual eyes as we observe the people around Jesus, and that we will see him more clearly too. Let's also pray that we will view our own lives through the lens of Jesus' love and sacrifice this Easter season.

A visionary blind man

Bartimaeus threw aside his coat, jumped up, and came to Jesus. 'What do you want me to do for you?' Jesus asked. 'My Rabbi,' the blind man said, 'I want to see!' (NLT)

Have you ever played one of those trust games where somebody leads you as if you are blind? How trusting were you? It's a bit scary, I admit. It's never easy when your vision becomes seriously impaired, but if it happens, you learn to rely on your other senses. My husband was registered blind in his mid-twenties and he 'sees' in a very different way from me. He listens intently and tunes into what is around him; he discerns the atmosphere and remembers his surroundings in extraordinary detail. He has a kind of vision and clarity that others sometimes do not have.

As we delve into this Palm Sunday scene, we read that as Jesus prepares to enter Jerusalem on a donkey, he passes a blind man who calls out to him. While many other sighted people could not see who Jesus really was, blind Bartimaeus can discern it clearly. Jesus asks him, 'What do you want me to do for you?' (v. 51). After hearing his plea, Jesus is able to restore what was lost to that trusting and faith-filled man so that his physical sight matches his spiritual insight.

As Jesus then turns to Jerusalem, he knows he is on the ultimate journey of restoration for all of us. But can we see him for who he really is today? Are we open to crying out to Jesus for our deepest needs like Bartimaeus did? This Palm Sunday, our Saviour still responds to us as we see him for who he really is. He restores us, renews us and ultimately reconciles us to God. That is definitely enough to make us open our eyes wide with wonder and shout Hosanna!

Thank you, Lord, for the way you see people and the way you see me. I pray that I would see you clearly again today and celebrate your goodness and mercy.

CATHY MADAVAN

A den of robbers

As [Jesus] taught them, he said, 'Is it not written: "My house will be called a house of prayer for all nations"? But you have made it "a den of robbers".' (NIV)

One year our family visited a city where cruise ships often stop for a few hours. We loved watching those giant floating communities come into dock, allowing their inhabitants to pour out on to dry land. What we didn't love so much was how the prices in the surrounding restaurants and shops inflated beyond all measure while the passengers were ashore!

Similarly, leading up to the Passover festival in Jerusalem, the temple sellers are apparently cashing in big time as the crowds pour into the area for this special religious celebration. Of course, it would have been entirely normal for animals to be sold for sacrifice as this was a sacred part of temple worship, but somehow these 'business people' have lost the plot about why they are there (to facilitate others worshipping God) and greed has got in the way.

This is a challenging story for all of us. Which of us has an entirely pure heart when we come to worship? But holiness clearly matters to Jesus, and this rare reaction from our Lord should speak to us clearly. We must never build a church, a ministry or a small group to advance our own ambitions, and we must ruthlessly guard against our own desires or creeping cynicism distracting us from why we do what we do. After all, they don't just affect us; they may also prevent others from getting closer to God.

It's telling that after this incident the crowds are amazed at Jesus' teaching. As the house of God was cleansed, so the power of God was clearly visible. Let's set our hearts on nothing less than building a holy 'house of prayer for all nations' (v. 17), as Jesus asks us to do.

Forgive me, Lord, when my reasons for serving or loving are less than pure. Draw close to me as I pursue righteousness and your beautiful presence above all else today.

CATHY MADAVAN

A self-sacrificing widow

'This poor widow has put more into the treasury than all the others. They all gave out of their wealth; but she, out of her poverty, put in everything – all she had to live on.' (NIV)

In our culture, we are quite used to people being hounded by the press. Celebrities and politicians know they could be subject to undercover reporters and so-called honey traps that cause them to dig their own reputational graves. But it seems there is nothing new under the sun. In preceding chapters Jesus, in his final days, was being tricked and tracked – not by the press, but by the religious leaders and teachers, who were trying to run theological and ethical circles around him in the hope they could catch him out and send him to the authorities for his comeuppance.

Jesus knows exactly what is happening. He warns his followers about these self-aggrandising leaders who flaunt their authority and soak up the adoration of others. Then he points out somebody totally different: a widow, whose offering to God of a couple of coins represents a level of sacrifice and worship that outweighs anything given by the wealthy and influential folk who take so much credit for their actions.

How typical of Jesus to point out not only what is beneath the surface of those pursuing him, but also the contrasting beauty of the kingdom of God, as demonstrated by those not normally noticed by others.

Jesus presents us with a topsy-turvy kingdom where character and devotion matter. Of course, the pharisaic law was there to enable believers to live righteous lives, but when we or the teachers of the law take credit for following those principles, even making a show of it, the heart of those principles has been missed. This widow reminds us to give whatever we can as generously as we can without making a fuss about it, because it is for God not for us.

Lord, help me to build holy habits for you. Show me how to honour you with all I have – my time, my money and my resources – so that my life gives glory to you alone.

CATHY MADAVAN

An extravagant woman

While [Jesus] was eating, a woman came in with a beautiful alabaster jar of expensive perfume made from essence of nard. She broke open the jar and poured the perfume over his head. (NLT)

I remember exactly which scent I was wearing on the day I got married. My husband-to-be had bought me a bottle of well-known perfume as a wedding present, which I am sure I must have liberally applied over myself and my white dress. Those of you who can remember the early 1990s will know the popular fragrances of the day were mighty enough to knock you out at 30 paces! Even to this day, if I smell that perfume it takes me back to the early years of our marriage. Our sense of smell is strongly connected to our memories.

So I wonder if, weeks after Jesus died, whenever people smelled the hair of this anonymous woman (possibly Mary Magdalene), or revisited the room where this fragrance-filled incident happened, whether the lingering smell brought back many memories of Jesus and their time with him. Of course, the significance of the moment she broke her jar and poured perfume over him would make sense in hindsight – she had metaphorically prepared Jesus for burial and prophetically anointed him as king in one act of humble extravagance. That is why, despite the extraordinary monetary worth of this sacrifice and the disapproval of others, Jesus commends her for her insight and for doing 'a beautiful thing' (v. 6, NIVUK).

Sometimes we too are surrounded by people who are jaded by cynicism or actively involved in betraying their faith, but just as this woman would always be remembered in the Gospels for leaving a sweet smell at a critical moment, so we can leave the fragrance of Christ wherever we are. It's a scent that lingers and points people to the goodness of God.

Where are you going to be today or tomorrow? What would the fragrance of Christ look and smell like there? How big a sacrifice would it be for you to pour out perfume for Jesus in that place?

CATHY MADAVAN

A traitor at the table

In the evening Jesus arrived with the Twelve. As they were at the table eating, Jesus said, 'I tell you the truth, one of you eating with me here will betray me.' Greatly distressed, each one asked in turn, 'Am I the one?' (NLT)

Have you heard of a trendy new experience where diners go to a mystery location for a secret meal that might be themed or contain certain challenges? I have a few brave friends who like to do such things. But of course for people who have to meet in secret organising mystery locations while full of fear is no dinner party at all.

As we join the build-up to the last supper, only two of the disciples know the location of the gathering, and only at the last minute. Tension is rising. The Passover festival is in full swing in a teeming city, but Jesus eagerly desires a significant and private meal with his followers, so sends them ahead to find a place.

The Passover was, and still is for Jewish people, a very holy festival celebrating the time when God spared the Jewish people from the plague of death and rescued them out of slavery in Egypt. By linking his own body and blood with Passover, Jesus explains that he is the new Passover sacrifice – he alone through his death and resurrection can atone for our sins and rescue us from slavery and death.

This rich symbolism is shared in the context of friendship, food and foot washing, but also tension. This holiest and humblest of meals includes Judas, who Jesus knows will lead him soon to a painful death. How does Jesus manage to wash the feet of Judas? How does he share bread and wine with him? Can you imagine it? Jesus always loves the unlovable. He is never selective. His sacrifice was and is for every person, and his offer of forgiveness extends to all. What a Saviour!

Thank you, Jesus, for welcoming everybody to your table. Forgive me when my thoughts or actions betray you, and help me to remember you and your sacrificial love today.

CATHY MADAVAN

A leader and a king

Pilate, afraid of a riot and anxious to please the people, released Barabbas to them. And he ordered Jesus flogged with a leaded whip, and handed him over to be crucified. (TLB)

Every day, assisted by a 24-hour-news cycle and social-media sites that beam breaking events instantaneously around the world, people on the ground can not only make the news but also send and shape it without authorities being able to do much about it.

Although there was no Twitter 2000 years ago, the crowd also shaped history in Jerusalem on Good Friday. The strength of their feeling clearly influenced those in authority, whatever the facts were. It's fair to say that Pilate, the governor of Judea, doesn't come across well here or in any of the Gospels. He presides over the trial of Jesus, finds no fault with him, then washes his hands of the decision by passing it back to the Jewish rabble, but signs his death warrant anyway. One leader's lack of conviction combined with people power led Jesus to the cross that day.

As Christians, we are surrounded by people who disregard our Lord and Saviour as irrelevant, and perhaps we have become used to the mocking voices of those in authority. Maybe some leaders in government would not defend the Christian truth because the crowd would shout all the louder. But make no mistake: Jesus' purposes are never thwarted despite what people may see or say. He knew God was in control that first Good Friday, and today we also trust in our faithful and merciful Father, who never abandons us. We know Good Friday is still very good news because King Jesus, through his painful sacrifice on the cross, offers us forgiveness and transformation and takes the sting out of death. Today is our day as a community and as individuals to declare to our world the news that Jesus is truly good.

If possible, read the rest of Mark 15 and observe Jesus before the chief priests, the religious leaders and the crowds, and crying out before his heavenly Father. Respond in prayer.

CATHY MADAVAN

A man of integrity

Joseph took the body, wrapped it in a clean linen cloth, and placed it in his own new tomb that he had cut out of the rock. He rolled a big stone in front of the entrance to the tomb and went away. (NIV)

When was the last time you were in a waiting room? I don't know who coined the phrase 'waiting game' because waiting never seems like much fun to me. Who wants to wait when there is so much else to do? However, sometimes we simply have to wait. There are seasons when health slows us down, redundancy presses the pause button, pregnancy grows our patience or bereavement puts life on hold.

Holy Saturday was a waiting day. The crucifixion was over, and we can only imagine the state of mind of all involved. We all wait differently, don't we? Some sit quietly and others get busy. Joseph of Arimathea, a wealthy man who was part of the Sanhedrin (but also a believer) takes responsibility, at some personal risk, for claiming the body of Jesus, wrapping it in linen and placing it in a tomb. What a man of integrity. The other religious leaders are also waiting, worried perhaps that the disciples might steal the body, and therefore placing guards around the tomb. The women closest to Jesus sit near the tomb – waiting.

I wonder which waiting room you are in today. It is significant to note that in this account, during the waiting, each person stays close to Jesus (albeit for different reasons). However we feel today and whatever we are waiting for, good or bad, the best thing we can do is stay close to Jesus. We don't ever know what is around the corner. We cannot always see the hope ahead. But we do know the One who gives us that hope. Let's wait on him today.

Heavenly Father, today I choose to wait on you. Teach me to be patient as I wait. Help me to reflect upon your faithfulness and to place my hope in you and your purposes.

CATHY MADAVAN

A worshipful woman

The women, deep in wonder and full of joy, lost no time in leaving the tomb. They ran to tell the disciples. Then Jesus met them, stopping them in their tracks. 'Good morning!' he said. They fell to their knees, embraced his feet, and worshipped him. (MSG)

As we celebrate this Easter day, declaring once again that Christ is risen, we follow in the footsteps of generation after generation of believers who have done the very same thing. How wonderful that is! However, the very first person to experience and meet the resurrected Lord Jesus was Mary Magdalene. This precious woman and her friend, whose testimonies would not even have been accepted as credible at the time, encountered Jesus in the garden that first Easter morning.

We know Mary was a devoted follower who provided for Jesus and supported him (Matthew 27:55–56). She was at his crucifixion, she watched his body being prepared for burial and she bought spices for embalming (Mark 16:1). She was Jesus' faithful follower and friend, but now she faces the powerful resurrected Lord. Her and her friend's response, having been told not to be afraid, is to worship him and clasp his feet. But Jesus asks them to go and share the news with the others.

This is a new chapter of life for them – an entirely new mission with new possibilities. I cannot imagine that any of the disciples had any idea what this would mean, but it was time for them to accept that death was no barrier for Jesus, and that God had an extraordinary plan for the world, which involved them.

As we celebrate the majesty and mercy of the risen Lord Jesus today, let's be inspired by Mary Magdalene and her friend and fall at his feet once more. Yes, he will send us out, and he has plans for us to transform the world in his name – but it begins with a devoted heart that leads us to worship first, then simply go wherever he asks us to go.

Hallelujah! He is risen! Thank you, Jesus, that you have beaten the grave and you are alive! Nothing is impossible for you. I worship and praise you, Lord, today.

CATHY MADAVAN

A road to hope

As they approached the village to which they were going, Jesus continued on as if he were going further. But they urged him strongly, 'Stay with us, for it is nearly evening; the day is almost over.' So he went in to stay with them. (NIV)

For years I struggled with the idea of hospitality. I had not been brought up in a home that had people over for meals, and I was thoroughly intimidated by the culinary brilliance of people who had invited us to dinner in the past. But I now realise hospitality is not supposed to be an episode of Masterchef. When we share somebody's home and spend time in their personal surroundings we see them differently. We get to know them in a deeper way. When we invite others in, even if they come with a bag of Indian takeaway, we are inviting them to intimacy. It's something we should do more often.

Soon after the resurrection, Cleopas and his companion are walking along the road to Emmaus, taking not only a literal journey but a spiritual one too. They had known Jesus. They are probably grief-stricken about the crucifixion. And yet they are prevented from recognising Jesus as he walks with them until they actively welcome him to stay with them. As Jesus breaks bread, they suddenly recognise him and realise he has risen from the dead. Their despair turns to joy and the word begins to spread.

I often wonder what would have happened if the companions had not urged Jesus to stay. Would they have remained downcast and unaware? It seems they experienced the blessing and honour of meeting their risen Lord as a result of welcoming him in. I wonder how open the door of your heart is today. Are you weary and disappointed, trying to cope on your own? Or is your life open to Jesus coming in? He wants to reveal himself to you and me again today. Let's welcome him in.

Sit somewhere comfortable. Imagine yourself inviting Jesus into the intimacy of your home and the reality of your life. Make him welcome. Ask him to reveal more about himself to you today.

CATHY MADAVAN

A doubting disciple

[Jesus] greeted his disciples and said to Thomas, 'Put your finger here and look at my hands! Put your hand into my side. Stop doubting and have faith!' Thomas replied, 'You are my Lord and my God!' (CEV)

In both the business and ministry worlds, we may hear people talk about 'early and late adopters.' Early adopters are enthusiastic entrepreneurs who sign up to and step out into a new and exciting plan almost before the person sharing the vision has finished their last sentence. Late adopters, however, take a little bit more convincing. They remain sceptical, waiting to see the evidence and how others are responding until finally they are convinced enough to place their eggs carefully into the basket. But when they do, they are often there for the long haul and utterly committed.

Thomas was one of life's late adopters. Everybody else may have been buzzing with the news about Jesus and his resurrection, but he was waiting for some hard physical evidence. In this passage we witness those doubts being met powerfully by Jesus, who knows we are all very different with diverse needs. However, Jesus also goes on to commend those who by faith declare him to be Lord even when they don't physically see what Thomas saw.

It's quite right that we all have different personalities and come to faith in unique ways – some based more on facts and others more on feelings. But Jesus asks us to put aside unhelpful levels of scepticism or pride as we walk the journey of faith. We are allowed to have our doubts (who doesn't?), because we are human and rational – indeed it is said that the opposite of faith is not doubt but certainty. But ultimately as Christians we walk by faith, not by sight, and when we don't have all the answers Jesus commends us for trusting in what is unseen but gloriously true.

Thank you, God, that you accept us with our doubts and weaknesses. Help me to put aside any unhealthy scepticism and to confidently grow in faith, hope and love.

CATHY MADAVAN

A fisherman's friend

Simon Peter said, 'I am going out to fish.' The others said, 'We will go with you.' So they went out and got into the boat. They fished that night but caught nothing. (NCV)

Every now and then my computer has a bit of a hissy fit and decides it no longer wishes to cooperate with my commands; it seems to take on a mind of its own and refuses to do what it is told. After trying everything I know (shouting, googling, turning it off and on again, and finally stroking it nicely) I take it back to its factory default settings – back to where it feels comfortable and starts working again.

While I would not normally compare people to gadgets, I do think we have our own default settings. We all have lines of thinking, attitudes or behaviours that we go back to when the chips are down and the shouting and googling have failed. Some of us get angry or start blaming. Others go shopping. Many start eating. Some of us find other ways of escaping or medicating the pain.

The disciples apparently had a default setting. When they had no idea what to do next, they went back to the beach and started fishing again. After years of witnessing the miraculous, travelling with Jesus and seeing God at work, they had lost their leader as they knew him and went to find a boat. They knew this place. It was probably comfortable and reassuring.

But then Jesus appears, disrupting their default settings and wonderfully redeeming them once more. He knows our escape places and can transform them into grace places that are no longer about fear but about freedom as he meets us there. Let's not resort to unhelpful, old ways of thinking, when instead we can create new default settings in which we look for Jesus in every circumstance.

When the going gets tough, where do you go? Consciously decide in prayer to make finding Jesus your new default setting in times of stress and uncertainty, or when making new plans.

CATHY MADAVAN

A restored vessel

The third time [Jesus] said to him, 'Simon son of John, do you love me?' Peter was hurt because Jesus asked him the third time, 'Do you love me?' He said, 'Lord, you know all things; you know that I love you.' Jesus said, 'Feed my sheep.' (NIV)

A while ago an artist friend of mine showed me a jar she had created. She had fashioned it after a Japanese kintsugi pot, which is distinctive because it is a vessel that has been broken and then patched together again using gold to seal and mend the breaks. While the brokenness is clear for the world to see, it is infinitely more valuable, physically stronger and far more beautiful following its restoration.

You don't need a special gift of discernment to see the breaks and mistakes in Peter. His passionate and impetuous nature was both his biggest asset and his biggest liability. Like all of us, he was a flawed human being. But in this passage, as we see him being lovingly and powerfully restored by Jesus in a way that brings beauty and worth to his previous denials and failings, we can find great reassurance. Jesus knew how valuable Peter would be to his purposes, and how, when full of the Holy Spirit, this fragile but significant human vessel would pour out the treasure Jesus had placed inside him (2 Corinthians 4:7).

Your story is also your glory when you allow your Creator God to mend you with his love and grace. Your cracks don't make you worthless – far from it. It has been said that we impress others with our success but we connect with them because of our vulnerability. It is the way you are being restored by God that gives others hope. So be prepared – whatever your broken and less-than-perfect pieces are, you are more valuable than you might realise, and God has not finished using you for his wonderful purposes yet!

Creator God, according to your word you are the Potter and I am the clay. I pray that you would continue to mend, restore, shape and use me for your glory so that others might come to know you.

CATHY MADAVAN

An apostle of love

Peter turned around and saw behind them the disciple Jesus loved – the one who had leaned over to Jesus during supper and asked, 'Lord, who will betray you?' Peter asked Jesus, 'What about him, Lord?' (NLT)

I wonder whether you were in the popular gang at school. I definitely was not. I had short, clipped hair, multiple braces, off-trend clothes and possibly the most embarrassing pushbike ever made, with a giant brown frame and tiny fat white wheels. It was nicknamed 'the tank'. Honestly, popularity was never an option!

It seems that even among the disciples there was a fair amount of argy-bargy about who was the greatest and the closest to Jesus. Certainly Peter, James and John were the inner three friends who witnessed some extraordinary moments with their leader. But even at this point, you can sense some rivalry from Peter in this passage. John, however, simply states that he is 'the disciple Jesus loved' (v. 20).

It's a startling transformation really. John was one of the sons of Zebedee who left his fishing business with his brother James to become one of the first disciples. Together they were called 'sons of thunder' by Jesus (Mark 3:17), from which we can conclude that they were probably fiery young men. So what transformed John into the writer who used the word 'love' more than the other Gospel writers put together? What changed this feisty fisherman into the intimate friend Jesus trusted to care for his mother after his crucifixion? What compelled this man to give up his life, to plant and lead churches, and to be persecuted and eventually exiled after the death of his Saviour?

The answer is clear: John was changed by Jesus. His personality and zeal were gifts to be redeemed and used for God's glory. Now he is remembered not so much as a son of thunder, but the apostle of love.

Lord, I'm sorry when I compare my relationship with you with how others know you. I love you, Lord. Thank you that you have no favourites and you love me and have called me to follow you.

CATHY MADAVAN

A command and a promise

'You will receive power when the Holy Spirit comes on you; and you will be my witnesses in Jerusalem, and in all Judea and Samaria, and to the ends of the earth.' After he said this, he was taken up before their very eyes, and a cloud hid him from their sight. (NIV)

Over these last two weeks, we have travelled with Jesus and the people who surrounded him, and now we leave this Easter season with Jesus' followers gathered around their risen Saviour one last time. Here they receive from him a command to wait for the Holy Spirit, and then a promise that they will be his witnesses throughout the earth.

In our culture, where obedience and self-discipline are hardly seen as attractive, it is important for us to gather together regularly around Jesus, his word and his people. We all rather like promises, but we also need to receive the commands. Jesus has called us to surrender our lives to him and follow him and his word in the power of his Spirit. We were never designed to go it alone; together we can remember who Jesus is, what Jesus has done and what he has asked us to do.

Equally, we need to encourage one another that as we surrender to his commands, we also receive his promises. As we walk in obedience, we can be sure we are part of God's great plans and purposes for this world. Every one of us is needed as witnesses for Jesus. As followers of Christ we are commissioned to bring hope, justice and freedom to those around us, and from where we are today to places beyond our imagination.

As Jesus ascended to glory, he placed his trust in us. It is for us to love him wholeheartedly, follow him closely, be empowered by his Spirit, stay united with our fellow Christians and share with compassion and boldness the truth about who Jesus is and the transformation he brings. What a wonderful privilege.

What has Jesus asked you to do? What has he promised you? Thank you, heavenly Father, for your Holy Spirit. Empower me to live for you today and every day.

CATHY MADAVAN

Zechariah – the people's return

Amy Boucher Pye writes:

Welcome to a fortnight with Zechariah, one of the minor prophets of the Old Testament. Before we start, I want to warn you that at times you may find the readings challenging and difficult. If this happens, you may be tempted to gloss over the biblical text. But if you stick with it, digging in, I think you'll uncover some riches that would otherwise lie buried. I believe the Lord blesses our efforts in seeking to understand his word, and he will help us in this task.

Zechariah was written about 520–518BC, when the Israelites had completed nearly 70 years of exile in Babylon, away from their home of Judah. They have finally returned to Jerusalem (Zechariah himself probably returned around 538–537BC), and not only is the temple in ruins but their practices of keeping to God's laws are in tatters. Zechariah speaks to the people through visions and prophetic words, calling them to return to the Lord with all their hearts and minds.

The task before them in the early chapters (1–8) is to rebuild the temple. They are to regain what they lost while in exile, but they must recommit themselves to the Lord. The final chapters (9–14) address the Israelites after they've rebuilt the temple, and speak of judgement for wrongdoing but also of the coming Messiah who will bring complete restoration. Some of Zechariah's prophecy contains apocalyptic language, which we may find difficult to interpret, but as we persevere we can come to more understanding.

Near the end of our fortnight together, we'll read about the Lord refining his people like silver and testing them like gold (13:9). If you find yourself struggling as you read, ask the Lord to show you how even engaging with Zechariah's prophecy can be a process of refining or testing. Ask him to bring you out of the experience as a pure precious metal, that you will shine forth with radiance and strength.

May our faith be enriched as we study God's word, seeking not only to understand it in its original context, but also how it applies to our lives today. May we search for the Lord expectantly, knowing that his word is 'alive and active', and 'sharper than any double-edged sword' which 'penetrates even to dividing soul and spirit' (Hebrews 4:12).

Are you ready?

Returning home

'This is what the Lord Almighty says: "Return to me," declares the Lord Almighty, "and I will return to you"… Then they repented and said, "The Lord Almighty has done to us what our ways and practices deserve, just as he determined to do."' (NIV)

I and my family arrived home feeling somewhat spacey from the overnight aeroplane journey and time difference. While we had been gone, we'd had a number of guests in our vicarage, as we'd been pleased to share our house. But our hearts sank as we saw that things were in disarray. Instead of sinking into the clean sheets I had requested and stretching out after a night squashed on a plane, I sighed and got on with making up the beds.

My example is admittedly minor, but it makes me wonder what the Jewish people were returning to in Jerusalem after 70 years of exile. They were coming home, but their city had been neglected and the temple destroyed. The land must have been overgrown, and any remaining buildings in a sorry state.

Their return home was physical, but the Lord is also calling them to return in their hearts. No longer are they to follow the practices of their ancestors, who did not serve God unreservedly, but they are to repent and honour the only true God. He wants them to love him with pure hearts, so he sends his prophet Zechariah to share not only his message of warning but also his promise of restoration.

We see in the second part of Zechariah 1 the first and second night visions, in which an angel shares with Zechariah God's words to his people. The Lord promises to return to Jerusalem and rebuild his house, and that he 'will again comfort Zion' (vv. 16–17).

Do you sense the Lord calling you to return to him? Or does your heart yearn for someone close to you who has left their earlier commitment to God? Spend some time asking the mighty yet gentle Lord to intervene, according to his mercy.

Lord, help me to return to you if I've gone astray. I love that you always run towards me as you welcome me back, your arms open wide.

AMY BOUCHER PYE

City walls

'Run, tell that young man, "Jerusalem will be a city without walls because of the great number of people and animals in it. And I myself will be a wall of fire around it," declares the Lord, "and I will be its glory within."' (NIV)

London is a sprawling metropolis. Locals speak of areas within London to distinguish where they live, such as Golders Green or Wapping. No walls enclose this sprawling urban mass, although of course centuries ago the Romans contained Londinium within walls.

Walls feature in the vision Zechariah sees of two figures who are concerned for Jerusalem. The first man comes with a measuring line, preparing for the task of building an enclosure around the city. But the angel who follows him declares, 'Jerusalem will be a city without walls' (v. 4). The Lord doesn't want to limit the growth of his city by keeping it hemmed in, because he will welcome people from many nations to live there (v. 11). And he himself will be their protection, a wall of fire around them (v. 5).

This image of the Lord being a wall of fire around his people is one I sometimes call to mind when praying for myself and others. Asking God to encircle us with fire helps us to acknowledge the unseen reality of the war between good and evil, between God and Satan. Now of course we don't need to overly fixate on this battle in the heavenly realms, thinking that everything negative is caused by demons. But we can offer a simple prayer affirming that the Lord is mighty as we ask him to burn a ring of protection around us.

The Lord is a wall around the city. How can you hold on to this truth today?

As you continue to consider walls, think before the Lord about any walls that hinder your relationship with a family member, a friend or an acquaintance in your community. How can you bring down these walls?

AMY BOUCHER PYE

Clothed in righteousness

Now Joshua was dressed in filthy clothes as he stood before the angel. The angel said to those who were standing before him, 'Take off his filthy clothes.' Then he said to Joshua, 'See, I have taken away your sin, and I will put fine garments on you.' (NIV)

When we come to an Old Testament passage like this, rich with prophecies that point to Jesus' coming, we may be tempted to bypass the text's meaning to the original reader. But we should consider Zechariah's vision in its context before applying it to its New Testament fulfilment.

We see in this vision a courtroom scene, with the high priest dressed in filthy rags. (The Hebrew word for these rags would have made the original reader think of excrement.) The high priest is therefore ritually unclean, so unable to enter the temple. But the Lord doesn't let Satan level his accusations against God's representative; instead he clothes him in fine garments and restores him to his presence. He has promised that he will not leave his people and that they will enjoy a time of peace as they 'sit under [their] vine and fig-tree' with their neighbours (v. 10).

For the people who had been living in exile, who had returned to a broken land, these words must have been a balm and an encouragement. They would no longer be left in filthy rags, but would be clad in robes fit for entering the temple. A time would come when they would enjoy peace and rest with the Lord.

Without losing the beauty of the words to the original reader, we can also revel in the way the Lord brings to fulfilment his promises through his Son Jesus. Jesus is 'the Branch' (v. 8) through whom God removed 'the sin of this land in a single day' (v. 9). As we welcome Jesus into our lives as our Saviour, he removes from us our filthy rags and gives us royal robes.

Consider what clothes you are wearing. How can you clothe yourself in 'compassion, kindness, humility, gentleness and patience' (Colossians 3:12) today?

AMY BOUCHER PYE

Symbols speak truth

'I see a solid gold lampstand with a bowl at the top and seven lamps on it, with seven channels to the lamps. Also there are two olive trees by it, one on the right of the bowl and the other on its left.' (NIV)

The healing properties of olive oil are discovered by many new parents. Our first baby had dry, flaky skin, and the only thing that helped was pure olive oil. As we rubbed it on him, we were tapping into just one of the manifold uses of this oil that has been used for millennia, as we see in Zechariah 4.

The prophet's fifth vision contains some intriguing images. As well as olive oil (v. 12), there is a lampstand and lamps, and there are olive trees and branches. The original recipients of Zechariah's vision would have associated the lampstand (in Hebrew, *menorah*) with the temple. A large *menorah* would have been lit there each day using only the purest olive oil, signifying God's light spreading throughout the temple and the world. In Zechariah's vision, however, there's no need for anyone to clean the *menorah*, as olive oil flows directly from the trees into the bowl.

In the Old Testament, the Lord often associates Israel with an olive tree, as in Jeremiah 11:16: 'The Lord called you a thriving olive tree.' In today's passage, the angel says the trees represent 'the two who are anointed to serve the Lord of all the earth'. These may be the prophets Haggai and Zechariah, who have been tasked with passing on God's message.

All these symbols would have spoken deeply to God's people, who were newly returned to Jerusalem and tasked with rebuilding the temple. The Lord reassures them that he will help them with this project – for he is the grand architect and supplier.

We may not be responsible for building a new church, but we can take encouragement from this passage that the Lord speaks to us through symbols and his Holy Spirit, and he will help us to worship him in ways that honour him.

Lord God, help me to worship you in truth, through your word and Spirit. May I come to understand your wisdom and live it out with grace.

AMY BOUCHER PYE

The curse of sin

The angel who was speaking to me came forward and said to me, 'Look up and see what is appearing.' I asked, 'What is it?' He replied, 'It is a basket.' And he added, 'This is the iniquity of the people throughout the land.' (NIV)

For a parent or carer, meting out punishment to children is not an enjoyable task. However, although it's tempting to ignore disobedience or wrongdoing, it's right to enact consequences for such behaviour. Christian parents or carers, considering the broader picture of the child's character, can ask God to shape him or her into his image and likeness.

The Lord punished his people when they turned from him. We see in the sixth and seventh visions the Lord judging thieves and liars and putting the wicked into exile. At the start of the passage we see a flying scroll, which represents the word of God. It's so large that no one can miss it, and it will be a means of judgement in the homes of wrongdoers.

As women reading this text, we may struggle with the sixth vision, in which wickedness is personified as a woman in a basket, and two women with wings take the basket to Babylon, a land away from God. But in ancient times, goddess worship was prevalent. The worship of Asherah, who was seen as a goddess of love and war, involved wanton sexuality and prostitution. So this vision fits with happenings in the culture of that day.

Also, some biblical commentators see a link between the woman in the basket and the great prostitute of Revelation 17, a woman 'covered with blasphemous names' (Revelation 17:3). She represents 'the great city that rules over the kings of the earth' (Revelation 17:18).

Today's chapter makes for uncomfortable reading, but I wonder if sometimes we sanitise ourselves from the consequences of wrongdoing. Perhaps grieving over the sins of the nations – and of our hearts – can bring forth repentance and a cry to God for help.

Lord, may you restore the reputation of women in society to reflect how you created women in your image. We seek to be pure in heart and committed to you.

AMY BOUCHER PYE

God with us

When the powerful horses went out, they were straining to go throughout the earth. And [the angel] said, 'Go throughout the earth!' So they went throughout the earth. Then he called to me, 'Look, those going towards the north country have given my Spirit rest.' (NIV)

This is the last of the eight night visions – perhaps you're relieved! The arrival of the four sets of horses signals that the visions are complete, because horses appeared at the beginning of the visions (1:8–11). They represent God's Spirit going throughout the earth and subduing the nations.

Zechariah swiftly moves from the heavenly visions back to what's happening on earth through the word of the Lord. Again the Lord wants to impress on his people the importance of rebuilding his temple, the place where his presence would dwell. He wants to return and live among them – not least to be with them in the years leading up to the coming of the Son of God.

God's words to Zechariah continue with an encouragement that his people won't be left as a small remnant, but if they continue to obey him, 'those who are far away will come and help to build the temple of the Lord' (v. 15). He reminds his people that his resources are not limited.

To me, this passage speaks of God's faithfulness as we wait. In hindsight we can see that God's people would need to wait a long time – over 500 years – for the Messiah. But as they wait, the Lord puts into place the means for them to worship him as they rebuild the temple. They will have a place to meet with him and be in his presence.

We often experience times of waiting in our lives, when the way forward isn't clear and we don't know what lies ahead. During those times, we can take encouragement from God's promises to his people, such as those he made through Zechariah.

Father God, enlarge my vision of you, that I might grasp how your resources are unlimited. May I have the privilege of helping you build your kingdom here on earth.

AMY BOUCHER PYE

Nearly there?

The people of Bethel had sent Sharezer and Regem-Melek, together with their men, to entreat the Lord by asking the priests of the house of the Lord Almighty and the prophets, 'Should I mourn and fast in the fifth month, as I have done for so many years?' (NIV)

Nearly two years have passed since Zechariah's night visions, and the people are in the midst of rebuilding the temple. They send representatives to the priests and prophets, including Zechariah, to seek the Lord over whether they should again take up the practice of fasting. On the surface this seems commendable, so we may be taken aback by God's response: 'When you fasted and mourned in the fifth and seventh months for the past seventy years, was it really for me that you fasted?' (v. 5). God sees through to their hearts and what lies underneath the question. As they reach the end of nearly 70 years of exile, they are basically asking, 'Are we nearly there yet? Is this time of exile coming to an end?' Despite the fact that they are back in Jerusalem, the exile continues in their hearts.

The Lord seeks not their rituals, but their purity of heart. He commands them to be just and care for the widows and the poor, and he laments how their ancestors ignored this requirement and turned from him, so he 'scattered them with a whirlwind' (v. 14).

How often do we find ourselves asking God midway through a project or a season of life, 'Are we nearly there yet?' We find the slog hard, as if we're trudging through mud, and we're tempted to give up. We plead with God to bring us to the end of the challenges. Sometimes he graciously answers our pleas, but sometimes he allows us to keep on squelching through. He never abandons us in the mud, but helps us with a strong arm when we feel weak. The mud may remain, but we know he is with us.

Lord God, at times I feel overwhelmed with the messiness of life. Keeping on with keeping on can feel so difficult. Give me strength, and help me to experience your life and peace.

AMY BOUCHER PYE

The joy of play

This is what the Lord Almighty says: 'Once again men and women of ripe old age will sit in the streets of Jerusalem, each of them with cane in hand because of their age. The city streets will be filled with boys and girls playing there.' (NIV)

As my husband and I enjoyed a meal in a restaurant in Spain, we watched a little boy at the next table shine with delight as he played with the condiments. Through his imagination he transformed commonplace packets of salt, pepper and vinegar into soldiers and captains. I realised anew that whatever country we live in, play is universal.

We see an unexpected picture of play in the first part of Zechariah 8. In the second of a series of promises opening with the words 'This is what the Lord Almighty says' is a declaration that the city streets will be filled with children at play (v. 5). As we read these encouraging words, we might feel they are out of keeping with the past judgement we encountered at the end of chapter 7. Biblical scholars believe they may be Zechariah's interlude between God's judgement and his blessings, helping the people to leave behind their wickedness as they embrace his favour.

This promise of joyful playing shows how the Lord will dwell with his people in Jerusalem, and how the weakest in society will feel secure in spending time in the streets. The Lord yearns for his people to live together in harmony.

Often we can feel so overwhelmed with the lists of things we need to accomplish in a day that we forget to rest, relax and even play. As we see in this vision, however, the Lord promises to bring us to a place of peace and contentment. Perhaps today we can spend some time relaxing and even playing, knowing that God is our loving Father.

Do you make time to play – to let yourself be silly as you laugh, or create, or relax? Try to carve out some time to play today, and later consider how you felt during and after your play session.

AMY BOUCHER PYE

A humble king

Rejoice greatly, Daughter Zion! Shout, Daughter Jerusalem! See, your king comes to you, righteous and victorious, lowly and riding on a donkey, on a colt, the foal of a donkey. (NIV)

As I took refuge from the burning heat of the Mediterranean sun among the palm groves in Elche, Spain – the largest such groves in Europe – I looked up at the spindly branches and marvelled at how thousands upon thousands of pilgrims to Jerusalem waved palm branches as they heralded the coming of their king, Jesus.

Zechariah's prophecies in chapters 9 to 14 can be seen as heralding the coming of Jesus. For instance, in today's passage the king arrives humbly, on a donkey (v. 9). Indeed, in their accounts of Jesus riding into Jerusalem, all four Gospel writers either name this prophecy or allude to it. Jesus didn't storm in on a war horse but rode a donkey, signifying that he was a different kind of king. He was not a political messiah who would save the Jewish people from the Roman occupiers, but a man who was God who would bring salvation. Though the pilgrims who waved their palm branches for Jesus were probably fuelled with nationalistic fervour, Jesus came to usher in the kingdom of God, not a new political structure.

Just as the original hearers of Zechariah's prophecy would have had no idea how it would be fulfilled eventually, Jesus' disciples only understood after his death and resurrection how he was a unique sort of king who came to rescue people from their wrongdoing.

We, like his disciples, can embrace Jesus' kingdom of grace, truth and new life, because when we receive his gift of freedom from our sins, we live in this new kingdom.

Why not take a few minutes to read the account of Jesus' arrival in Jerusalem in John 12:12–16. Think how the man who was God humbled himself to ride a donkey, and ushered in a different kind of kingdom.

AMY BOUCHER PYE

Living water

Ask the Lord for rain in the springtime; it is the Lord who sends the thunderstorms. He gives showers of rain to all people, and plants of the field to everyone. (NIV)

Water – it's the stuff of life. It makes up over half our bodies, and we need it to stay alive. We wash in water; we water our crops with it; it slakes our thirst. We simply can't exist without it.

The Lord uses this everyday liquid to remind his people that he is their source of life. He tells them, through Zechariah, to ask him for rain to water the earth and give life to the plants that feed them (v. 1), and that false gods only 'give comfort in vain' (v. 2). Even if the Nile dries up (v. 11), they will live securely in his name, strengthened by him (v. 12).

Today or tomorrow why not think about God your provider every time you use water in some way? For example, when you boil a kettle, remember that he loves you. When you wash your hands, recall that he is the good shepherd who knows his sheep, in contrast to false idols who leave the people wandering (v. 2). When you flush the loo, think about how he restores his people (v. 6). When you look outside and see rain or mist, ponder how God makes his children joyful (v. 7).

Thinking about something as ordinary as water can refocus our attention on the all-powerful yet all-loving God who made us. As we acknowledge that all things come from him who is our living water, we drink and are refreshed.

I have friends who are mission partners in Niger, working to build wells for a fresh water supply for the people they serve. How could you extend the gift of water to someone?

AMY BOUCHER PYE

The good shepherd

I shepherded the flock marked for slaughter, particularly the oppressed of the flock. Then I took two staffs and called one Favour and the other Union, and I shepherded the flock. (NIV)

Enacted parables are one way God speaks truth to his people. For instance, at times in the Old Testament we see the Lord asking his prophets to enact a sign on his behalf. It happens twice in today's chapter. Both 'sign-actions' portray shepherds and illustrate to God's people why foreign rulers are oppressing them.

In the first sign-action, God asks Zechariah to shepherd his flock (vv. 4–14). Zechariah soon grows weary of those who detest him (v. 8), just as the Lord found his people's disobedience tiresome. As a way of illustrating the breaking of the covenant, Zechariah snaps his staffs of Favour (v. 10) and Union (v. 14). As payment he receives 30 pieces of silver, the price of a slave, which is also the amount Judas received for betraying Jesus.

The second sign-action continues the warning over God's displeasure about the way his people aren't staying true to him. Though he is the good shepherd, they are following worthless shepherds who will sacrifice their own sheep, roasting them on the spit (vv. 16–17).

Passages such as John 10:1–21, where Jesus says he is the good shepherd, are all the more meaningful when we read them in the light of texts such as this. Through his sacrifice as the perfect lamb, Jesus has brought us into sweet communion with God. It's as if on the cross the staffs have been miraculously repaired, and once again we enjoy his Favour and Union.

Lord God, you are the good shepherd who lays down his life for his sheep. You speak to me, and I know your voice. Help me to follow only you.

AMY BOUCHER PYE

Times to come

On that day, when all the nations of the earth are gathered against her, I will make Jerusalem an immovable rock for all the nations. All who try to move it will injure themselves. (NIV)

Apocalyptic literature can be difficult to decipher. We've probably heard of the self-professed prophets who declare a certain date to be the last day of the world. When that day comes and goes, they revise the date, and so on. But although this type of writing about the end times can be difficult to understand, we can benefit from studying it. And this is what we'll engage with in the final chapters of Zechariah and his last prophecy.

Zechariah speaks of God moving mightily in the future to establish his kingdom, but his people will experience trials as they, for instance, see horses struck with panic and riders with madness (v. 4). But those in Jerusalem will be saved, as a testament to God's power and goodness. Their salvation will reflect God's mighty hand.

With the benefit of hindsight, we can also see in this text rich applications to the coming – and second coming – of Jesus. In ancient times, piercing someone almost certainly meant they would die. Therefore the parallels between 'the one they have pierced' (v. 10) and Jesus are clear (see John 19:34).

As we have noted previously, Zechariah's prophecy applied to the people to whom it was first given, and it continues to speak to us today.

Take some time to reread today's chapter prayerfully, and consider some of the war-torn areas in the world. As you read and pray, ask God to make his people like an 'immovable rock' (v. 3) and a cup out of which God's grace flows.

Father God, we don't always understand your words about the end times. Reveal to me just what I need to know for this hour and this day, as I trust in your goodness and grace.

AMY BOUCHER PYE

Refiner's fire

'This third [of the people] I will put into the fire; I will refine them like silver and test them like gold. They will call on my name and I will answer them; I will say, "They are my people," and they will say, "The Lord is our God."' (NIV)

I've never seen silver being refined, but I remember touring the House of Waterford Crystal factory in Ireland. It was fascinating to see the crystal being shaped in the scorching heat, which was a key part in the process of making the special glass so beautiful. When silver or gold are refined by heat, impurities are left behind and the result is strong, shiny metal.

We see in Zechariah's vision of the end times that the Lord will refine his people, cleansing them from their sins and removing those who are impure (vv. 1–3). No more will idols get in the way of worshipping the true and living God (v. 2), and the sheep not of the shepherd's pasture will be scattered (vv. 7–8). Those remaining will be refined 'like silver and [tested]… like gold' (v. 9). But God will never leave them, for when they cry out to him, he will answer them, reassuring them that they are his people (v. 9).

When we sweat in the heat of the fire, we can quickly be tempted to think we're alone, or that God doesn't hear us and doesn't care. But if we hold firm to our faith while in the furnace, we'll see our confidence in God grow and flourish. In retrospect we can see that his hand was on our lives, even though at the time we may have felt abandoned. And when we next face testing times, we can remember his faithfulness and goodness as we ask for strength to hold on.

'You, God, tested us; you refined us like silver… we went through fire and water, but you brought us to a place of abundance' (Psalm 66:10, 12).

AMY BOUCHER PYE

All made holy

On that day 'holy to the Lord' will be inscribed on the bells of the horses, and the cooking pots in the Lord's house will be like the sacred bowls in front of the altar. (NIV)

Zechariah's prophecy ends with a fascinating glimpse of the times to come. Not only does it paint a picture of the city of Jerusalem in redeemed form, but it reveals some of the hardship and bloodshed that will occur as God effects his justice. We might find those passages more difficult to read and ponder.

Some of the images here correlate with the pictures of the end times in the book of Revelation. Zechariah says, 'On that day living water will flow out from Jerusalem, half of it east… and half of it west' (v. 8). In Revelation we see the river of life flowing down the middle of the holy city (Revelation 22:1–2). In Zechariah we see a lack of distinction between day and night (vv. 6–7), which Revelation 22:5 echoes: 'There will be no more night.' And there will be one Lord, and one Lord only – the 'king over the whole earth' (v. 9).

Unique to Zechariah's prophecy, however, is the interesting final paragraph in which cooking pots 'will be like the sacred bowls in front of the altar' (v. 20). All that is everyday and ordinary will be made holy and welcomed into God's house, and even things that have been declared unclean will be made clean. God's holiness through his presence with his people will spread throughout the city.

What a vision to behold! We can believe God will bring about his plans of redemption and restoration when he makes all things new. Though we face disappointment and heartache in this life, God's light shines through the cracks, bringing us hope and strengthening our faith as we welcome his kingdom on this earth as in heaven.

What an amazing God you are! Thank you for your revelation to Zechariah, and for our engagement with it. Set firmly in my mind and heart the truths you want me to hold on to from this your word.

AMY BOUCHER PYE

Letter to the Hebrews (part 2)

Rosemary Green writes:

Earlier in these notes (21 January–3 February) we spent two weeks grappling with the writer's challenge to Christians from a Jewish background. In the face of persecution they were tempted to draw back from following Jesus and revert to their Old Testament worship and practices. The author longed for them to stay faithful to Christ, and demonstrated powerfully Christ's superiority to the angels, to the prophets, to Moses and to Joshua; in Christ we have a better covenant, a better sacrifice and a better high priest than under the old ways. We tried to see both how the Jewish Christians thought, and how the author of this letter wanted them to think.

In these last three chapters in Hebrews we move into (mostly!) calmer theological waters. However, whereas I used to look on chapters 11 to 13 as a stand-alone section for all Christians, I now see the continuity with the earlier chapters. The author wants to show that our life of faith in Christ builds on the faith of the past and also supersedes it. Seeing the context has really excited me. It has given me a deeper understanding of these chapters, and a fresh appreciation that the more I know of the Old Testament, the better I can grasp the richness of the New. This has enhanced my desire to follow Christ unswervingly and wholeheartedly.

We live in an era when Christians are marginalised and scorned in a way that hasn't happened in Britain for centuries. It is easy for our clear convictions to be diluted and eroded by the prevailing sceptical, often hostile, climate. This makes Hebrews even more relevant to us.

One thing is worth explaining: when the writer quotes from the Old Testament, he may use the Septuagint. This is a translation of the Old Testament from Hebrew to Greek that was made in the second century BC, and it is patchy in quality. Sometimes the quotation is scarcely recognisable if you look up the verse in your own Bible. Not surprisingly, both quotations from and allusions to the Old Testament are frequent. Sometimes Christians would like to stick to the New Testament and not bother with the Old. But our grasp of the New will be very sketchy if we know nothing about the Old.

Read on with expectation and joy!

Faith in action

Now faith is confidence in what we hope for and assurance about what we do not see. This is what the ancients were commended for. (NIV)

Have you ever received the comment, 'I wish I had your faith'? People often think faith is a static object that can be put in a box and held. But faith is an active word, reaching out to grasp something we believe reliable. We exercise faith when we sit down, trusting the chair to hold our weight. A child exercises faith in jumping off a high wall, trusting a parent's safe hands for the catch. Faith makes the connection between the present situation and the future expectation.

So the author says in 10:38, 'My righteous one will live by faith. And I take no pleasure in the one who shrinks back' (Habakkuk 2:4, from the Septuagint). The encouragement is to go for it; go forward, not back; and remember the saints of old. Then the author launches into chapter 11, and reminds his readers of many Old Testament saints whose active faith was based on the living God, not on the temple practices these Jewish Christians are tempted to maintain.

The author puts before us some of the 'ancients' (v. 2) of the early chapters of Genesis, such as Cain and Abel. Why was Cain's offering unacceptable to God? The story can puzzle us, but it reminds me of God's X-ray eyes; he saw the seeds of jealous anger in Cain's heart. Enoch lived a life of faith and obedience, in step with God. Noah built the ark, obeying God, probably in the face of ridicule during a drought. The faith of the latter two meant they responded obediently to God's leading.

Faith moves forward; fear retreats. I have heard it said that faith is spelt R-I-S-K. Are you confident enough in the trustworthiness of your God to take risks in obeying him?

ROSEMARY GREEN

Faith as a way of life

By faith Abraham, when God tested him, offered Isaac as a sacrifice. He who had embraced the promises was about to sacrifice his one and only son, even though God had said to him, 'It is through Isaac that your offspring will be reckoned.' Abraham reasoned that God could even raise the dead. (NIV)

'Abram believed the Lord, and he credited it to him as righteousness' (Genesis 15:6). Faith was the supreme mark of Abraham's life, from when he first left Ur, to when he later left Harran, where they had settled, to go south to Canaan. Faith was his way of life, except for a couple of blips – first when he lied about his wife, and later when he got Hagar pregnant. Even the mightiest of saints have their cracks – a thought that can be my encouragement, but mustn't become my excuse, in my own failures.

Some phrases strike me in this commentary on Abraham's life. First, 'when called' he 'obeyed and went' (v. 8). I have experienced my own lesson on the folly of disobeying God, and of procrastination. One June the Lord told me to straighten out a friendship that was dominating my life. I replied, 'Yes, Lord, I will – when the autumn programme starts.' Between June and September that friendship crashed, causing pain to many people. I didn't obey God, who had made his wishes plain. Not so Abraham. He obeyed 'even though he did not know where he was going' (v. 8). Faith obeys the trustworthy God who knows the future.

Second, 'he lived in tents... looking forward to the city with foundations' (vv. 9–10). Tents speak of impermanence – but Abraham's life was safe, because, like the hoped-for city, 'its architect [was] God' (v. 10).

More than ten years ago I was privileged to visit Billy Graham in his home. He had been recently widowed, and had failing hearing and eyesight, but above his fireplace was written in German, 'A mighty fortress is our God'. Even in his weakness, that's where Billy Graham's trust – like Abraham's – lay.

Abraham, and even the sceptical Sarah, had seen 'the impossible' in Isaac's conception and birth. Later, Abraham trusted God for 'the impossibility' of restoring his son to life. How far do I trust that same God?

ROSEMARY GREEN

Keep going

All these people were still living by faith when they died. They did not receive the things promised; they only saw them and welcomed them from a distance, admitting that they were foreigners and strangers on earth. (NIV)

Think first what these verses meant to those who first read this letter – the Christians from Jewish backgrounds, tempted to revert to old ways. The writer continues his look back at Israelite history in order to encourage them to keep going steadily with Christ.

Jews are strong on remembering the past. I first visited the Holy Land in 1959. I saw burnt-out tanks beside roads, left from the 1948 war with the Arabs, and I visited the Holocaust Museum in Jerusalem, remembering the six million Jews killed by the Nazis. At the same time the development in Israel, a state only eleven years old, was remarkable.

Through the incidents referred to in verses 20–29 the writer is saying to the Jewish Christians, 'Yes, you may be finding life difficult now. So did your forebears. They coped with uncertainties and challenges by looking forward, trusting in a God who would take them through into the future. They didn't look back to the past. They looked ahead to the fulfilment of God's promises, whether on earth or in eternity.'

What should these verses mean to us? Everyone reading these notes is unique; no two situations are identical. For some, life is going smoothly and immediate problems are small. For others, life is discouraging and there are battles on many fronts: in marriage, in divorce, with children (young and adult), at work, in unemployment, with housing, in friendships, in health. But isn't the message the same now as then? God is bigger than all of these. He will stand by you. Time and again God promises, 'Don't be afraid, for I am with you' (Genesis 26:24). He sustained the saints of old; he will sustain you now. Trust him to take you forward into the future.

Lord, thank you that we have the example of these Old Testament believers who trusted you. Please help me to keep going in faith, even when my situation doesn't change.

ROSEMARY GREEN

People of faith

These [people] were all commended for their faith, yet none of them received what had been promised, since God had planned something better for us so that only together with us would they be made perfect. (NIV)

The story of remarkable men and women of faith over many centuries continues. Some are named; others are not named but their stories are easily identifiable (such as Daniel in the lions' den; Shadrach, Meshach and Abednego in the furnace, etc.). Others are more obscure (with many of their stories in apocryphal rather than biblical literature). Some were victorious, clearly triumphant in their faith. Others underwent torture, flogging, imprisonment and violent death.

They all had one thing in common: they 'were all commended for their faith, yet none of them received what had been promised' (v. 39). They didn't give up, either in victory or adversity. Neither must we, says the author to the flagging Christians of 2,000 years ago. We're in this together.

In 2018, we belong to the same fellowship, the same community of faith, as these believers. We are in it with them. And we have two huge advantages that they lacked: Jesus' example to follow and the power of the indwelling Holy Spirit.

This chapter recalling the active faith of saints many centuries before Christ leaves me with this thought: faith looks to the future but helps us live in the present. Our living God promises reward and fulfilment in an eternal future, whether or not the reward comes in our lifetime on earth. But however tough our situation, however hard the struggle, he gives us strength and endurance to keep going in the present.

Each morning my husband and I read together from *Daily Light* (**www. crosswalk.com/devotionals/dailylightdailypath**), which puts together Bible verses on a theme. Recent encouragements included 'Cast your burden on the Lord, and he will sustain you' (Psalm 55:22, ESV).

Thank you, Lord, that you are always ready for me to cast my burden on you. Help me to trust you for tomorrow as I share today's burdens with you.
ROSEMARY GREEN

Focus on Jesus

Let us run with perseverance the race marked out for us, fixing our eyes on Jesus, the pioneer and perfecter of faith. For the joy that was set before him he endured the cross, scorning its shame, and sat down at the right hand of the throne of God. (NIV)

Do you remember, as a child in the school gym, trying to walk steadily along a narrow beam? If your eyes looked straight ahead, fixed on a stationary target, there was a chance of staying upright. But if your eyes strayed sideways or downwards, wobble and collapse were inevitable. That's today's picture: keep your eyes fixed on Jesus. He stayed steadfast, though his suffering, in life and in dying, was far worse than any his followers undergo.

Think about the structure of this letter to the Hebrews. First are the complicated chapters on how Jesus is way better than the worship practices they had under the old covenant (the 'shadow' that God instituted, as preparation for Christ (10:1)). Then, in chapter 11, we have the example of a multitude of ordinary men and women down the ages, whose faith in God for the future sustained them when their present was bleak. In today's verses we have Jesus' supreme example in the face of opposition and pain.

I first met these verses in my early days as a 'real Christian'. I was a student when my faith came alive. In my traditional church upbringing I had never questioned the historicity of Jesus' virgin birth, miracles, death and resurrection. It was mild background warmth to my life. Firewood had been laid in the fireplace, as it were, with my head knowledge of Jesus providing the paper and sticks. Then, in my first weekend at college, I recognised my need for Jesus' forgiveness and friendship. I invited his Spirit into my life: that was the match that lit the fire! I remember my mother couldn't understand my new enthusiasm: wasn't what she had taught me enough? Sometimes I was unwise in my zeal, and we clashed. I had to learn to run the long-haul race, with my eyes fixed on Jesus.

Sing or say prayerfully: 'Turn your eyes upon Jesus. Look full in His wonderful face. And the things of earth will grow strangely dim in the light of his glory and grace' ('Turn your eyes upon Jesus' by Helen H. Lemmel (New Spring)).

ROSEMARY GREEN

Painful but fruitful

[Our fathers] disciplined us for a little while as they thought best;
but God disciplines us for our good, in order that we may share in his
holiness. No discipline seems pleasant at the time, but painful. Later
on, however, it produces a harvest of righteousness and peace. (NIV)

'This hurts me more than it hurts you!' has supposedly been said by parents in the past when disciplining their children – and not believed by the children, I'm sure! 'It's not fair,' the children mutter (or shout!). Parents are human and make many mistakes. How I wish I could do many things over again, differently, with my children.

But our heavenly Father is never unfair. I love Deuteronomy 32:4: 'His works are perfect, and all his ways are just. A faithful God who does no wrong, upright and just is he.' His discipline is genuinely for our good, 'that we may share in his holiness' (v. 10). If wood could feel it wouldn't enjoy rough sandpaper rubbing its surface, but it might appreciate how smooth it was afterwards.

The two biggest spiritual transformations in my life, after my conversion, came out of discipline. After 20 years as a Christian, my spiritual life had become very hollow. Then came a fantastic month spent in South Africa – a holiday for the family, a preaching tour for my husband. However, he developed meningitis and was hospitalised in Durban, while I had to take the children back to England, and school. During that time God lifted me out of my drabness into a new love for Jesus. A friend commented three weeks later, 'One day you will be able to see blessing come out of this.' My reply: 'Don't worry; I know it already!'

Years later I got into a habit of allowing my anger to erupt furiously whenever I felt wronged or let down. As a consequence I was set aside for a period from all church ministry, which was very painful. But God used that time to spring-clean me of my deep-rooted anger and its manifestations. New peace and new confidence followed, and now I thank God for the friends who cared enough to confront me.

'Wounds from a friend can be trusted' (Proverbs 27:6) if we allow God to use those wounds to change us, refine us and grow his holiness in us.

ROSEMARY GREEN

Hints on holiness

Make every effort to live in peace with everyone and to be holy; without holiness no one will see the Lord. See to it that no one falls short of the grace of God and that no bitter root grows up to cause trouble and defile many. (NIV)

I wonder what image the word 'holiness' brings to your mind. It might conjure up a picture of a prim, meek and mild Victorian spinster out on charitable errands to the poor. I recently read the biography of Lilias Trotter, born in 1853, who, in 1888, as a single lady with ill-health, went as a pioneer missionary to Algeria. There's nothing meek and mild about that!

Look at Jesus. He is anything but meek and mild. He shows us all the purity, power, dynamism, flexibility, love and humour of the godhead. That is divine holiness!

These verses select a few aspects of practical holiness. 'Make every effort to live at peace with everyone' (v. 14). Don't be too hard on yourself when your relationships are not perfect. We are responsible for ourselves; we are not responsible for other people.

'Make every effort… to be holy' (v. 14). 'Every effort' – that is a high standard. Sometimes, despite an early morning prayer for holiness, I find I have failed dismally two hours later.

'See to it that no one falls short of the grace of God' (v. 15). How can I help others to understand and live in the light of God's free, totally undeserved favour?

'See to it that… no bitter root grows up' (v. 15). Roots of unforgiveness easily grow into bitterness and are hard to eradicate. The roots damage the person who harbours them, friendships, marriages and whole churches.

Beware of sexual immorality. Beware of greed. Genesis 25:27–34 tells us how Esau's desire for instant gratification overcame his concern for the birthright of spiritual blessing reserved for the oldest son.

Our mistakes can be forgiven, but that does not necessarily undo their long-term consequences.

Strengthen your weak knees (pray and pray some more!) and live in holiness.

ROSEMARY GREEN

God's holiness

You have come to Mount Zion, to the city of the living God, the heavenly Jerusalem. You have come to thousands upon thousands of angels in joyful assembly, to the church of the firstborn, whose names are written in heaven. You have come to God, the Judge of all. (NIV)

Moses and the Israelites had to learn first of all the supreme lesson that God is a holy God. He is not to be taken lightly. He is pure, unapproachable and untouchable. He demonstrated his awesome holiness and majestic power to the Israelites, showing he was to be feared and obeyed.

God's holiness has not changed. He is still the judge of all. But we see another side to him, because we are confident that Jesus is 'the mediator of a new covenant' (v. 24). We have the privilege of coming close to him.

The writer paints a lovely picture of the joy of fellowship in heaven. The closest, most loving, most joyful, most worshipful fellowship we ever experience on earth is a very pale reflection of the unimaginable glory and joy of heaven.

But I sometimes think that, through our very confidence in being able to approach God and call him Father, knowing he forgives us, we have lost some of our awe, wonder and respect for the one mighty God. Perhaps the current casual overuse of the word 'awesome' speaks of a loss of awareness of the might and majesty of God.

In the light of the exultation in heaven, the author's words of warning are his sternest yet. 'If they did not escape when they refused him who warned them on earth, how much less will we, if we turn away from him who warns us from heaven?' (v. 25). 'Please, Christians in the first century,' he says, 'please don't turn back on all Jesus gives us.'

The plea is as strong now as when it was written. Please, Christians in 2018, please don't turn back on your commitment to him.

Father, how I thank you that I can indeed call you Father, and that I can come close to you. Please restore in me a deep reverence for your holiness and majesty.

ROSEMARY GREEN

Practical living

Now may the God of peace, who through the blood of the eternal covenant brought back from the dead our Lord Jesus, that great Shepherd of the sheep, equip you with everything good for doing his will, and may he work in us what is pleasing to him, through Jesus Christ. (NIV)

The writer touches on many practical topics at the end of this 'briefly' (!) written letter. They seem quite disconnected: love's outworking in caring for others; marriage, money and trust; leadership; false teaching; and sacrifice and suffering.

You might like to pick one paragraph that particularly links with your situation. Read it again, and ask God to make some phrase stand out for you. Chew it over. What is God saying to you for your own life? Ignore anything else I have written for the moment; focus on your one thought.

Here are my scattered comments to accompany the author's scattered thoughts. For a start, verse 3 struck me. I have been thrilled to learn something of the ministry in local prisons. Prisoners are becoming Christians and finding the power to overcome addictions. Pray for them; they need solid inner change to enable them to live stable lives when they are released.

Marriage is under enormous pressure in modern society, as it is redefined in our culture. One man with one woman for keeps is mutually enriching – but rarely entirely easy. Pray for Christian marriages to shine as beacons; pray for those you know who are starting marriages, and for those whose marriages are struggling.

Finally, look at verses 20 and 21. Who is God? He is the God of peace, and Jesus is the great Shepherd. What has he done? Jesus' death and resurrection bear fruit now and in eternity. What will he do? He will give us all the resources we need to live in ways that please him.

What a wonderful God we have!

Lord, thank you, thank you, thank you for your generosity, your power and your constant presence. May I live to please you.

ROSEMARY GREEN

Recommended reading

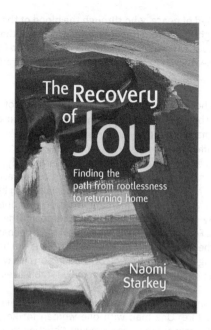

This book weaves story and Bible reflection to trace a journey that begins in rootlessness and despair and takes a wanderer across the sea to a series of islands. These islands are the setting for a succession of events and encounters through which emerge a progression from that initial rootlessness, through healing, to a rediscovery of the joy of feeling at the centre of God's loving purpose for our lives.

The Recovery of Joy
Finding the path from rootlessness to returning home
Naomi Starkey
978 0 85746 518 4 £6.99
brfonline.org.uk

musings of a clergy child
growing into a faith of my own

Nell Goddard

Nell Goddard writes honestly and openly about the ins and outs of growing up in a Christian home, from her experience as the daughter of two vicars. With hilarious anecdotes, tough lessons and spiritual reflections from wrestling with faith, this book charts what it's like to live in the goldfish bowl of a vicarage, grow up in the shadow of your parents, lose your faith and find it again.

Musings of a Clergy Child
Growing into a faith of my own
Nell Goddard
978 0 85746 546 7 £7.99
brfonline.org.uk

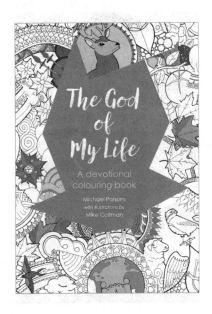

Doodling and colouring help many of us to be present in the moment, giving us more focus and aiding concentration. This unique book offers the chance to colour while reflecting on a psalm and so to concentrate unhurriedly on our relationship with the Lord. Many will find this book a helpful resource for a special kind of devotional time.

The God of My Life
A devotional colouring book
Michael Parsons
978 0 85746 584 9 £8.99
brfonline.org.uk

To order

Online: **brfonline.org.uk**
Tel.: +44 (0)1865 319700
Mon–Fri 9.15–17.30

Delivery times within the UK are normally
15 working days. Prices are correct at the time of
going to press but may change without prior notice.

Title	Price	Qty	Total
The Recovery of Joy	£6.99		
Musings of a Clergy Child	£7.99		
The God of my Life	£8.99		

POSTAGE AND PACKING CHARGES			
Order value	UK	Europe	Rest of world
Under £7.00	£2.00	£5.00	£7.00
£7.00–£29.99	£3.00	£9.00	£15.00
£30.00 and over	FREE	£9.00 + 15% of order value	£15.00 + 20% of order value

Total value of books	
Postage and packing	
Total for this order	

Please complete in BLOCK CAPITALS

Title .... First name/initials .... Surname...

Address...

.... Postcode..................................

Acc. No. .... Telephone ....

Email...

Please keep me informed about BRF's books and resources ❑ by email ❑ by post
Please keep me informed about the wider work of BRF ❑ by email ❑ by post

Method of payment

❑ Cheque (made payable to BRF)   ❑ MasterCard / Visa

Card no. ⬜⬜⬜⬜ ⬜⬜⬜⬜ ⬜⬜⬜⬜ ⬜⬜⬜⬜ ⬜⬜⬜⬜ ⬜⬜⬜⬜

Valid from ⬜⬜ ⬜⬜ Expires ⬜⬜ ⬜⬜ Security code* ⬜⬜⬜

MM YY   MM YY   Last 3 digits on the reverse of the card

Signature* .... Date .... /.......... /..........
*ESSENTIAL IN ORDER TO PROCESS YOUR ORDER

Please return this form with the appropriate payment to:

BRF, 15 The Chambers, Vineyard, Abingdon OX14 3FE | enquiries@brf.org.uk

To read our terms and find out about cancelling your order, please visit **brfonline.org.uk/terms**.

Each issue of *Day by Day with God* is available from Christian bookshops everywhere. Copies may also be available through your church book agent or from the person who distributes Bible reading notes in your church.

Alternatively you may obtain *Day by Day with God* on subscription direct from the publishers. There are two kinds of subscription:

Individual subscriptions
covering 3 issues for 4 copies or less, payable in advance (including postage & packing).

To order, please complete the details on page 142 and return with the appropriate payment to: BRF, 15 The Chambers, Vineyard, Abingdon OX14 3FE

You can also use the form on page 142 to order a gift subscription for a friend.

Group subscriptions
covering 3 issues for 5 copies or more, sent to **one** UK address (post free).

Please note that the annual billing period for group subscriptions runs from 1 May to 30 April.

To order, please complete the details on page 141 and return with the appropriate payment to: BRF, 15 The Chambers, Vineyard, Abingdon OX14 3FE

You will receive an invoice with the first issue of notes.

All our Bible reading notes can be ordered online by visiting
biblereadingnotes.org.uk/subscriptions

For information about our other Bible reading notes,
and apps for iPhone and iPod touch, visit
biblereadingnotes.org.uk

All subscription enquiries should be directed to:
BRF, 15 The Chambers, Vineyard, Abingdon OX14 3FE
+44 (0)1865 319700 | enquiries@brf.org.uk

DAY BY DAY WITH GOD GROUP SUBSCRIPTION FORM

> All our Bible reading notes can be ordered online by visiting
> **biblereadingnotes.org.uk/subscriptions**

The group subscription rate for *Day by Day with God* will be £13.50 per person until April 2019.

☐ I would like to take out a group subscription for .... (quantity) copies.

☐ Please start my order with the May 2018 / September 2018 / January 2019* issue.
I would like to pay annually/receive an invoice* with each edition of the notes.
(*delete as appropriate)

Please do not send any money with your order. Send your order to BRF and we will send you an invoice. The group subscription year is from 1 May to 30 April. If you start subscribing in the middle of a subscription year we will invoice you for the remaining number of issues left in that year.

Name and address of the person organising the group subscription:

Title .... First name/initials .... Surname ....

Address ....

.... Postcode ....

Telephone .... Email ....

Church ....

Name of Minister ....

Name and address of the person paying the invoice if the invoice needs to be sent directly to them:

Title .... First name/initials .... Surname ....

Address ....

.... Postcode ....

Telephone .... Email ....

Please return this form with the appropriate payment to:
BRF, 15 The Chambers, Vineyard, Abingdon OX14 3FE

To read our terms and find out about cancelling your order, please visit **brfonline.org.uk/terms**.

The Bible Reading Fellowship is a Registered Charity (233280)

DAY BY DAY WITH GOD INDIVIDUAL/GIFT SUBSCRIPTION FORM

To order online, please visit **biblereadingnotes.org.uk/subscriptions**

☐ I would like to give a gift subscription (please provide both names and addresses)
☐ I would like to take out a subscription myself (complete your name and address details only once)

Title .... First name/initials .... Surname ....

Address ....

.... Postcode ....

Telephone .... Email ....

Gift subscription name ....

Gift subscription address ....

.... Postcode ....

Gift message (20 words max. or include your own gift card):

....

....

Please send *Day by Day with God* beginning with the May 2018 / September 2018 / January 2019 issue (*delete as appropriate*):

(please tick box)	UK	Europe	Rest of world
1-year subscription	☐ £16.95	☐ £25.20	☐ £29.10
2-year subscription	☐ £30.90	N/A	N/A

Total enclosed £ .... (cheques should be made payable to 'BRF')

Please charge my MasterCard / Visa ☐ Debit card ☐ with £ ....

Card no. ☐☐☐☐ ☐☐☐☐ ☐☐☐☐ ☐☐☐☐

Valid from ☐☐ ☐☐ Expires ☐☐ ☐☐ Security code* ☐☐☐

Last 3 digits on the reverse of the card

Signature* .... Date .... /....... /.......

*ESSENTIAL IN ORDER TO PROCESS YOUR ORDER

Please return this form with the appropriate payment to:
BRF, 15 The Chambers, Vineyard, Abingdon OX14 3FE

To read our terms and find out about cancelling your order, please visit **brfonline.org.uk/terms**.

The Bible Reading Fellowship is a Registered Charity (233280)

DBDWG0118